Vocal Wisdom

Vocal Wisdom

ENLARGED EDITION

Maxims of

Giovanni Battista Lamperti

Transcribed by
William Earl Brown

Supplement edited by
Lillian Strongin

A CRESCENDO BOOK

TAPLINGER PUBLISHING COMPANY

NEW YORK

Published in the United States by
TAPLINGER PUBLISHING CO., INC.
P.O. Box 175
Marlboro, N.J. 07746

Fifteenth printing. Printed in the U.S.A.

ISBN   0-8008-8022-6 cloth
        0-8008-8023-4 paper

(Previously ISBN   0-87597-085-0)

DEDICATION

To the memory of my Master, Cavaliere Giovanni Battista Lamperti, the last great master of the old Italian manner of singing.

WM. EARL BROWN.

PREFACE TO THE ENLARGED EDITION

When my late teacher, William Earl Brown, died in 1945 he willed all his musical effects to me.

Among the many manuscripts I inherited, was a little black note-book containing a record of Mr. Brown's lessons with Lamperti in Dresden, Germany, in the years 1891-1893.

These notes, written in French, were dictated to Mr. Brown by Lamperti and are in Lamperti's exact words. I have translated these notes and they are now printed for the first time in this enlarged edition.

In addition to these notes, I have included a few selected essays from Mr. Brown's manuscripts.

I trust the note-book and essays in the supplementary section will be helpful and inspiring.

Lillian Strongin

1957
New York

PREFACE

WE strengthen our own idea when we find another agreeing with us.

Nevertheless, I consider it unwise, nay, even fatal, to be over-influenced by another's opinion, unless we are prepared to take it in understandingly. When it coincides with, or completes our own reasoning, we have found a feather of truth.

It is wise, however, to take note of things we do not agree with, without antagonism. To-morrow, or in two seconds, they may be just the ideas we have sought so long.

Life is too brief to work out a problem of art alone. We should profit through another's experience and research, avoiding his faults while emulating his virtues.

All roads lead to Rome.

A fact can be approached from all sides.

Listen and learn, but trust yourself, for you must go your path and not another's.

Select from the topics in the book any subject of interest to you personally.

My deductions and explanations may help you to find your voice.

W. E. B.

INTRODUCTION

THERE was a Golden Age of Song. This period produced the greatest singers of all time, re-reflecting the art of the greatest masters of any period. These teachers made few rules, but insisted on obedience to natural laws, which were physical, not anatomical. The ear, not the muscles, guided both master and pupil, though strenuous gymnastics of breath and voice were insisted on.

These exercises did not constitute a "method," nor were they intended to be followed in the final use of the voice. They were simply "setting-up" movements. Each teacher and every singer had his own way of developing the voice. Therefore no definite system of *bel canto* has descended to us, except advice by word of mouth, from singer to singer.

Most of these streams of admonition have dried up. There is one, however, that to-day is full and strong— the simple precepts of the Lampertis, father and son. The father heard these rules from the great singers and composers of the past—Rubini, Malibran, Presto, Bellini, Donizetti, Rossini, among others of this golden span. The son imbibed the ideas from his sire. Many of us are "carrying on" these traditions of our beloved master Giovanni Battista Lamperti, the man who taught Sembrich, Stagno, Bellincione, Hastreiter, Edyth Walker, May Stone, Agnes Huntington, Radcliff-Caperton—the list is too long to write here.

I have ventured, in a volume, to interpret and elucidate the maxims and teachings of this last great master of singing, with whom I was associated many years, as pupil and assistant.

These aphorisims are not intended to be gulped at one or two sittings; my book is not written to be read casually. Rather than attempt to build a "system" or a vocal "method" on the ideas of the master, I have preferred to set down as faithfully as I could, with the help of the note-books I filled during my years with him, these succinct paragraphs. Out of these fragments which I have grouped in some slight semblance of order, the knowing reader may find the master key to a score of vocal "methods."

The traditions and precepts that developed the great voices of the Golden Age of Song have descended to me *viva voce* from this master.

This wisdom came down the centuries to me; I pass it on to you.

Through your guardian hands it will reach generation after generation.

Help me to spread abroad the ideas in which you have so great a share, thus becoming my assistants as well as my beloved pupils.

WM. EARL BROWN.

New York.

TABLE OF CONTENTS

*PREVENTING THE DECADENCE OF THE ART OF SINGING

By G. B. LAMPERTI

HERE has never been so much enthusiasm for the singing art, nor have there been so many students and teachers as of late years.

And it is precisely this period which reveals the deterioration of this divine art and the almost complete disappearance of genuine singers and worse, of good singing teachers.

What is the cause of this? How can it be prevented? By a return to the physiology of singing.

Just as the lack of good dramatic singers who can sing *Semiramis* or *Norma* becomes apparent, to a like degree do we find a lack of good singers who can sing *Donna Anna* or *Oberon*.

One part of the lay-world says that there are no longer real voices, and the other that there is no longer any talent. Neither is right. Voices still exist, and talent too, but the things which have changed are the *study of the breath, of vocalization* and *of classic rèpertory*, as cultivated by the singers of former times. They used to study for four or five years before they dared to be seen publicly in a small rôle.

<hr />

* EDITOR's NOTE: These thoughts of the Master are so applicable to contemporary conditions that I am presenting this article in full. And Lamperti penned this article in 1893!

Nowadays, after maltreating the larynx for a few months, a student considers himself an artist, and attempts the most difficult feats. Neither Verdi nor Wagner has ever said to singers: "In order to sing our music it is not necessary to study the art of singing; it is sufficient to have a strong voice and to be a good actor." On the contrary, when Verdi talked to the Congress at Naples on the decadence of music, he said that it was absolutely necessary to return to the serious study of former times.

But in Germany it is not only the true sopranos who have almost disappeared but also the tenors, because a German tenor who cannot sing Wagner cannot obtain an engagement or position of importance. Therefore the singers strain their voices: they force themselves in order to sing the Wagner rèpertory.

It would be much better, if tenors who did not possess the vocal resources for Wagnerian opera would refrain completely from singing that rèpertory. The Wagnerian operas demand powerful tenors who can sing the recitative with pompous voice; nevertheless, tenors who possess only pretty, fresh, agreeable but weak voices, insist on singing Wagner. They do this without a previous thorough *study of the breath,* of *solfeggio* and *vocalization,* and without any comprehension of *voice registers.*

A tenor possesses the most delicate type of voice: it demands a very earnest and carefully prepared course of study. But most tenors in Germany sing with the emission of a baritone because they then believe themselves to be Wagnerian tenors. They force the middle voice and do not realize that the maltreated voice will, with time, become old and tired.

I remember having heard a tenor named Pardini in Italy who at seventy-two years of age sang the *Otello* of Rossini. He still had the fresh voice of a young man. The tenor, Stagno, who I permitted to make his début in 1860 at Genoa, has been singing the last thirty-two years. "Cavalleria Rusticana" was written for him—he has sung the whole rèpertory of Wagner, Meyerbeer, Verdi, et al; yet he still maintains his fresh voice, as do others such as Negri, Companini and Tomagno.

Why are the voices of Patti and Madame Sembrich so well preserved?

Because they sing only the rèpertory which suits their voices.

In 1885 I was in Paris in order to assist Sembrich at her début in "Traviata" and "Lucia." One day she told me that she would like to sing "Faust." I protested energetically and urgently advised her to sing only the operas of her rèpertory. (She would have ruined her voice in "Faust" and in a short time would have become a singer like thousands of others.)

This period is swayed by a prejudice: everyone says the music of Verdi and Wagner spoils the voice. That is not true of perfected voices. And here we have the one cause of the deterioration of singing, which no one will grasp and which nevertheless is so simple. The insufficiently cultivated voice, which possesses neither the flexibility nor the art of the breath-supported legato, naturally quickly wears itself out.

Let us make a comparison: is a person who is strongly drawn to the piano necessarily a virtuoso? No, to the desire must be added serious study, in order to completely develop into artistry.

Therefore, how can one expect that the voice (which is the most beautiful, but at the same time the finest and most delicate instrument) will reveal all the passions of the soul without thorough study of its technique?

It is a pity that young singers, who are studying voice, immediately sing songs and arias, literally before they know how to open their mouths, instead of earnestly studying the real support of the voice (the mechanism of the breath) in order to develop the voice and to make it smooth and flexible.

Certain teachers are mainly at fault in that they take advantage of the inexperience of pupils, to the disadvantage of the art of song.

In my opinion, it is not absolutely necessary for a singer to have a big voice, nor even a pretty one: if one just acquires security of breath, purity of enunciation and legato, any voice will sound agreeable to the ear. Never more than of late, have the gymnastics of the breath and smoothness of tone (legato) been neglected by teachers of singing. And precisely these two things are the chief requirements of a singer and of those who wish to undertake the important position of a singing teacher.

In spite of the fact that modern music for light sopranos is devoid of the coloratura of the time of Mozart and Rossini, it is a necessary principle to again add the gymnastics of the breath, the larynx and the smoothness of tone (legato).

Without this study the art of good singing would in a short time become a chimera. Not until a singer knows how to control the breath and unite his tones is he equipped easily to convey every variety of expression which is demanded by the new composers; to hold the tone longer (as one can with a violin or violoncello) and to give to songs the *nuance* and color which dramatic art permits.

The foundation of all vocal study lies in the control of the breath.

The technical development of the voice is brought out by the double functioning of the lungs, which consists of: first, inhaling the breath noiselessly; and secondly, making use of the diaphragm to control the breath as economically as one pleases, in order to leave the vocal apparatus completely independent. (The diaphragm is a muscle on which the lungs rest and which is indispensable to singing.)   Once one becomes master of the organs of breathing, one can begin the study of legato.

Legato means the carrying of the voice or the imperceptible merging of one tone into the other.   Between one tone and the next the breath may not be interrupted, but must be held as though the tones were one.   But in passing from low to high tones, the breath must take the opposite direction from the voice.

Without these precautions, one can neither sing legato nor achieve a pure coloratura, which would otherwise remain deficient or jumpy (*cavallina*). The control of the breath is the support of all vocalization.

It is possible to end phrases and cadenzas so that there will be a residue of air in the lungs.   It is a great mistake to end a phrase with collapsed lungs.

The stroke of the glottis (violent attack) which many singing teachers advise, is absolutely harmful to the voice, and it is wrong to use it in order to begin a phrase well; one can easily in time develop a harmful or fatal inflamation of the larynx.

It is desirable for a student to follow certain hygienic principles.

Among other things he should talk little and not loudly, not sing immediately after meals, deny himself butter and other rich foods, practice with full voice, but reasonably and with rest periods. He should study before a mirror, in order to acquire a pleasant expression and never lift the shoulders, etc.

If the pupil has the weakness of holding his tongue high or keeping his teeth closed, the mirror is the only way to overcome it. I strongly advise refraining from the use of artificial devices, placing objects in the mouth, on the tongue or between the teeth, etc. These are playthings whose uselessness has been sufficiently proved by experience. In singing, one should not "cock an ear" to listen any more than one does in speech. Through such efforts the muscles of the throat easily become rigid.

Beginners also often make the mistake of "letting themselves go" while singing because they believe it achieves good results; that is untrue. The head must always be cool, only the heart should be warm.

The language best suited for the study of singing is Italian, because it is the only one without aspirates. The music which I prefer for vocalists is that of the masters Rossini, Mozart, Bellini, Weber, Donzietti, et al.

It is absolutely necessary for a pupil who wishes to devote himself to the study of singing, to choose a teacher from the very beginning who has made certain studies on the use of the voice and all aids of the breath. He must be absolute master of the legato, and be able to demonstrate it in order to carry over his knowledge to his pupils in all its branches and details.

Of course it is not necessary for the teacher to possess a splendid voice, but to the highest degree he must understand the art of imparting technical details to his pupils. In addition there must be a reciprocal magnetic attraction between pupil and teacher, which helps to convey ideas from teacher to pupil. The teacher must have a profound knowledge of the aids to a properly cultivated mechanism, and ability to impart this knowledge to his pupils. The teacher should hypnotize the pupil with his knowledge.

A great loss to the melodramatic art is the disappearance of *opera-buffa* and *"semi-seria"* (romantic opera), such as, for instance, "Don Pasquale," "The Marriage of Figaro," or "Linda di Chamounix," etc. In former days we developed true artists with such a rèpertory.

Those who were endowed with a robust voice and a truly dramatic talent discovered the truth of this after singing for several years in the comic or romantic operas, going through the *"tirocinio."* (*Tirocinio* means going through everything from the beginning thoroughly and practically.) Not until then could they offer their services in dramatic operas. These singers were then ripe (*provetti*) and thorough (*profondi*) artists of their medium.

The public tires of the "Barber," "Cosi Fan Tutte" or "Fra Diavolo" only if it is poorly done.

Now I ask, why do the modern composers not write good comic or romantic operas instead of imitating Wagner or Verdi? That would be a help to the renascence of the art of singing.

Often the cause of poor performances of art-operas is the conducting. When "Lohengrin," "Walküre," "Aida" or "Otello" is not being performed, no care is given to good color, good scenery or singing technique. No one bothers to see whether the singers are equal to their tasks. Finally in the small operas, the costumes are old and the whole performance of terrible frigidity. The effect of the opera is entirely lost. The critics blame the work. The director should honestly reply: "I, the conductor, have not used sufficient care. The singers are incapable of singing these melodies without support from the instrumentation, because we no longer possess the knowledge and ability of real singers. That is the reason why these performances actually arouse pity."

In spite of all this, it is my firm belief that we should not retrogress further. It is only necessary for the young composers to realize that they are not Wagners or Verdis who can write a "Tannhauser" or

"Aida" as a first creation. For their own good and the good of art, they should write operas of modest proportions. The success of Mascagni's "Cavalleria Rusticana" has proven this most decidedly.

It is wrong to believe that after studying the Italian method of singing (the one and only true method of good singing) it is impossible to interpret and sing dramatic music.

Were not Malibran, Pasta, Grisi, Sonntag, Cruvelli and Cattalani great dramatic and technically sublime singers, who excelled equally in *Norma, Otello, Semiramis,* and similar rôles?

If these singers had been contemporaries of Verdi and Wagner, as they were of Bellini and Rossini, they would have been technically complete and at the same time truly dramatic singers, who could have sung "Norma" and "Die Walküre," "Aida" and "Semiramis" equally well.

One must not confuse the term "dramatic interpretation" with a vulgar demonstration or exaltation which forces the voice and exaggerates the gestures which accompany it. Unfortunately this is often seen even in artists of the present time, who do not consider themselves dramatic singers.

Richard Wagner says in his writings on Madame Schröder-Devrient, "She had no 'voice,' but she knew how to control her breath so perfectly, and to permit a truly womanly spirit to issue forth so wonderfully, that one thought neither of singing nor of voice, as one listened."

Only he who understands correct singing can obtain real power and expression in song, whether he sings Italian, French or German music. There are only seven tones in the scale, and it is equally difficult to sing them in any language, so that they will be agreeable to the listener, and conserve the voice.

In these times, when the demands of the singing art are growing vague, let us return to a study of physiology and the *older* Italian method!

These remarks are, of course, not a "method." They simply explain the causes of the decadence of singing as I have observed them in an experience of many years.

LAMPERTI MAXIMS

Quiet Throat

THE larynx does not rise to produce a high pitch. The backward tipping of the cricoid-cartilage secures the upper tones of voice.

For low tones this ring-shaped cartilage tips forward to normal position, leaving the throat quiet, as in speaking.

Though the larynx need not be held muscularly fixed in one position, for either upper or lower register, it should remain quiescent throughout a song. This repose is a sign of physiological action of the throat.

The throat, however, does alter its shape somewhat for vowel and volume. But diction takes care of that.

A quiet throat is the result of interrelation of vocal energy and breath power.

There is an affinity between voice vibration and breath like the relation between string vibration and bow.

THE MOST DIFFICULT PROBLEM

HE most difficult problem in singing is to prolong and swell a tone at a given pitch, making a *messa di voce*.

For the voice instinctively wants to rise or fall (inflect), even in speaking.

And therefore scales and arpeggios are easier than monotone phrases.

Release of breath-energy and vibration of a voice seem the same in producing a sustained tone as it does in singing a florid cadenza, no jumping of throat, nor rigidity of neck muscles.

When a tone is prolonged at a given pitch, it should have its internal life—like a flame,—fed by the inherent energy of breath.

Any use of muscle (other than to release energy) vitiates the tone by disturbing its overtones (divisional vibrations, called harmonics).

"A tone must be self-starting, self-prolonging and self-stopping," said Lamperti.

To make this possible, complete management of breathing is an indispensable necessity.

Generally, faulty singing is caused by awkward respiration. In fact all bad habits of the throat are merely efforts of protection against clumsy management of the breath.

DESIRE AND REFLEX

O-ORDINATED activity of body and brain, spontaneously started, sustained and stopped by the phonation of the voice, is the ultimate goal of the singer.

The voice becomes master.

It begins a sound at any pitch, on any word, with any consonant, or any vowel—in fact with any vocal utterance—at its own pleasure.

Though coming from the throat, the singing voice seems as independent of it as the speaking voice appears to be.

The mechanism in the throat does not have to consciously change for pitch, nor for register to either speak or sing.

Of course this is true only when continuous co-operation of body and brain obtains.

Do we not soon learn to use our fingers to manipulate things—even the typewriter and piano—and to perform the innumerable daily duties of the hands?

Thought and muscle are schooled until instinct and reaction develop and take command. Then what was arbitrary becomes automatic.

Singing is a natural use of the voice. But to learn to play on the larynx demands training of brain and body until desire and reflex control the process. Then that which was difficult becomes easy.

Mental and physical gymnastics must of necessity be specific in order to stimulate and sensatize the various parts of brain and body. But these methodical exercises should not be confused with final singing because they inhibit nature's instinctive processes.

Actual singing becomes a subconscious co-operation of the multitudinous activities of the whole personality when perceptions of music, language and breathing ripen into realizations.

Realizations of the rudiments of melody and harmany, of the sensations of words in head, mouth, throat and chest, and of the inherent energy in the breath, could make of an orator a singer.

In fact an orator has as much technic as a singer, but he has no realization of what to do with it when he tries to sing.

No more "method" is needed to sing than to speak. But singing does demand definite realizations and co-ordinate activity that stimulate desire and reflex.

INTROSPECTION

REATHING and singing gymnastics are beneficial only when they impel concentrated attention.

Mentally anticipating internal sensations of word, tone and timber, as well as interior activities that produce them leads to control of the voice

Examining your own thoughts and feelings, while singing, until you know what is taking place in brain and body is the only procedure.

To acquire this conscious knowledge of mental and physical phenomena of song demands the utmost searching introspection.

Do not listen to yourself sing!

Feel yourself sing!

When internal conditions are right and ready, the singing voice appears—not before.

THE MATURE VOICE

ONLY in due time does the fruit of an endeavor ripen. This is so true of the endeavor to sing, that few voices ever come to maturity, through haste to be heard. The facile voice that might grow to maturity by arduous study, seldom ripens, but remains incomplete. The difficult voice oft arrives at mechanical control through sheer effort, but the tone remains unpleasant, lacking mental direction.

The physiological singing tone evolves from the speaking voice. Its ripening depends on the activity of all parts of the body and all functions of the brain. Phonetic vibrations felt at lips, nose, head, throat and chest, carry distinct messages to every part of the body. These messages are recorded in the singer's consciousness until habitual reaction takes the place of effort and thought.

Though the sense of hearing educates the singer musically and phonetically, the sense of feeling (touch) organizes him vocally.

The physiological singing tone takes its own time to ripen. When fully grown it is both dark and light, filling head, throat and sometimes chest.

READY TO SING

HAT is the sensation of being ready to sing? It is a subjective feeling associated with the insistent desire to sing!

Like that of a "tight-rope walker" as he steps on the wire;

Like that of the swimmer as he ceases efforts and trusts the support of the water;

Like that of the diver, the moment before beginning his plunge;

Like that of the listener who hears a mysterious sound in the quiet of the night;

Like that of the sharpshooter the instant before he pulls the trigger;

Like that of the archer the instant before he releases the arrow;

Like that of the violinist when about to start his performance;

Like that of the expert whistler just before he makes a sound;

Like that of the juggler at the beginning of his act;

Like that of the dancer as he rises on his toe;

Like that of the orchestra conductor, with his bâton poised in the air;

Like that of the orator as he opens his lips before the waiting audience:

All these acts demand objectively, a potent vitality,

conscious, accurate control of energy, and complete knowledge of the thing attempted.

When you are sentient from head to foot and know your song, then you are ready to sing.

OVERTONES

THE singing voice is born from the overtones of regular vibration of the vocal-cords. Those harmonics nearest the pitch sung form the major triad. All diatonic and chromatic tones are reproduced by the higher divisions.

When a tone is pure, the lower, harmonious overtones only are heard in the voice.

When the voice is forced, the higher discordant harmonics predominate, causing hard, metallic, sharp quality.

When overtones are lacking the voice sounds hollow, sepulchral, wooden.

Sensitive co-action of the whole muscular and nervous energy is the condition demanded for the production of pure tone.

As the student's ideal of tone grows the latent powers in nerve and muscle respond until every cell in the body is joyously doing its duty.

The ear leads "clairvoyantly" and recognizes the real spark that kindles the voice.

We must work and wait, for this does not take place as a result of method, but appears of its own accord when conditions are right.

Singing depends on the sense of hearing.

The physical ear perceives and knows how pure tone sounds in voices and even in musical instruments.

The mental ear "visions" little by little how to produce it.

Singing is instinctive.   Its control is subconscious.

Fundamental exercises are only to make the body and imagination more supple and sensitive, to respond to the desire to produce a beautiful tone and sustain a melody.

A teacher can only reveal ourself to ourself.

We must keep to his fundamentals (if proved true) but trust our own initiative.

No two minds react in the same way.

Our knowledge and power come only from our individual reactions and realizations—on them our progress depends.

The human being is the most perfectly adjusted musical instrument in existence.

Most great singers know very little or nothing about their vocal organs and lungs—and are largely self-taught.

Each has a different idea of "how he does it" and

that "method" is not exactly like the one his master taught him.

The fact is—each voice is a law unto itself.

Working It Out Alone

ANY noted singers have such fear of teachers and methods that they prefer to "work it out" alone.

A celebrated singer said to me, "I studied with —————— in Europe (one of the most eminent teachers) and found him a wonderful man for 'style.' Had I continued his 'method,' I would have ruined my voice."

A famed soprano is gradually losing her voice—not by bad singing but by "coaching" with too many "voice doctors." Each teacher gives her some new trick—and little by little undermines the power and control nature gave her.

Jenny Lind when young, lost her voice. Failing to regain it by a prolonged study with Garcia in Paris, she went home and "worked it out" and became the greatest singer of her age. Her ideals were so high, she was often found in tears for the many faults she had committed during a performance.

All that Patti knew about her method was "to keep her tones from being breathy."

A great baritone educated his voice by eradicating the faults he heard in his phonograph records.

One of the most eminent dramatic sopranos "found herself" only after singing light rôles for twenty years.

A white-haired woman, she is still singing.

Another great artist sang baritone parts, (inadequately) until the age of forty, when he "found" his head voice, and became the greatest living tenor.

Sims Reeves was a boy soprano. After his voice changed, he became a basso profundo; later a baritone; and finally the most noted of English tenors.

I heard him sing gloriously at the age of seventy.

Too Many Teachers

IF we find our voice by ourselves or with the help of a master, we must not try other methods. It is fatal. "I have studied with ten different teachers," said a student proudly. "That is nine too many," exclaimed Lamperti.

The motives and movements of your mind and body make only half of the proposition of singing. Natural phenomena of vibration and resonance constitute the other half.

You will discover these phenomena of phonetics in pronouncing words.

You find control of motives and movements in the reactions from uttering these words on melodies.

Only the voice that develops from the germ (initial vibration) to the full-fleshed sound (resonance) will last. This is from the feet, up.

After the voice is developed, stop thinking of the growing years, and sing from the head down.

The presence of resonance in head, mouth and chest (overtones) is proof that your voice is full-grown, full-fleshed.

Thereafter you get ready to sing from your head downward, because your head is the instrument.

Your head, mouth and chest are hollow or resounding with tone all the time. Never dissipate the hollow feeling. Breathe through it.

Never sing from your throat up.

You might as well try to lift yourself by your bootstraps.

SOME POINTS

THE "dissolving" of one vowel into another without mouthing and the "passing" from exhalation to inhalation without jerking, are two earmarks of good singing.

Breath is "held back" by two fundamentals, vibration (pulsating of the vocal lips) opposing the exit of compressed air from the lungs, and concerted action of entire muscular covering of the body restraining the energy of the escaping air, the diaphragm acting as a "stop-cock."

While sustaining a good easy tone, open mouth as in a yawn; it excites upper chest and throat activity. Begin and end with teeth closed. If the beginning and end of your tone feel the same—undisturbed—the gymnastic is beneficial. If the vibration of the voice "breaks" during the stretching, the exercise is hurtful. This exercise will make you realize that vibration is controlled in the pelvis, resonance in the chest and head.

All atoms of the elastic body linked together, continually in action with a minimum of movement and effort may be realized by the perseverent student.

If the top falls out of your tone, you have uprooted your energy from the pelvic region.

If resonance disappears, you have lost the muscular connection between head and chest.

If your tone is breathy, your diaphragm is relaxed. Its use is to release or restrain the imprisoned breath power, but never let it escape as air.

If your tone is pinched, you are pushing loose breath against the vocal-cords. The dynamic force in compressed breath, not muscular effort "supports" the voice.

If your tone is too far back in your mouth, enunciation is at fault.

If your attack is too hard, you are hitting your tone from beneath your throat instead of focusing it above the vocal-cords. You are "striking the glottis" instead of attacking your tone.

A muscle continues its activity only when a necessity compels it to do so. Continuous tonicity of muscles is excited by continuous mental and emotional stimulation.

The pitch of the voice must depend on tuning the vocal-cords, and not on power of the breath which furnishes energy only. It is the harnessing of this breath power to prevent interference with vibration, yet furnish all degrees of audibleness to the tone, that takes years of hard work, and continual practice.

Your voice must have an inexhaustible supply of both regular vibration and breath-power for each phrase, and you must be able to renew both without observable interruption of rhythm, tone or diction, while keeping continually co-ordinated.

You cannot sing well, until your least "hum" excites your whole co-ordination as much as your loudest tone. You cannot sing with your mouth open if you cannot do so with it shut.

Do not be discouraged when an exercise loses its efficacy. Change to another. Then come back to the one that became "stale."

A muscular action is but a gymnastic unless it be a reaction to mental or emotional stimulation.

There is no dividing line between thought and emotion.

But there may be a preponderance of one or the other.

50-50 is a safe mixture.

Until you know the equivalent physical sensation of the sound mentally imagined, you are never sure of making the effect you desire. Every sound is mirrored in head, throat and chest.

There is nothing so meaningless as a mechanically controlled tone, although it be emotional. It lacks beauty.

Because inherent energy in compressed air secures both pitch and power of tones, the singer feels the "control" of breath descend in the body as the voice ascends the scale or increases in volume. Even soft singing and diminishing volume of tone demand pelvic control of breath.

Coloring or shaking tones, using effusive or explosive effects, etc., at the expense of balance between voice and breath is detrimental to progress and the health of the larynx.

Not anatomical dissection, nor physiological vivisection, but natural functions of respiration, phonation, hearing, feeling, seeing, etc., make the physiological foundation of singing. All else is "excess baggage."

THE GOLDEN RULE OF SINGING

T is through our desires, our sensations, our perceptions, that we gain control of our activities in body and mind.

This is especially true in singing.

Our acts are fashioned by our ideals of melody, harmony and poetry.

No ideal is ever realized because it changes to higher or lower quality as we near it.

Thus we are ever striving onward or sinking backward, whether we will or not.

A friend, a book, a word, a look may help or harm us.

We disintegrate if we take on a harmful suggestion.

We integrate when we adopt a helpful hint.

We know what is beneficial or deterrent if we consider the result of a deed before we do it.

We find by experience (our own or another's) what is hurtful or helpful.

Ideals, though never reached, are easily toppled from their heights.

A destructive thought will do it.

When they fall, we drift with any tide.

Constructive thinking will uphold them.

As long as they remain we need not fear.

Then unashamed, unafraid, undeterred, we can climb the heights of achievement.

To know the result before we act is the "golden rule" of singing.

When your tone emerges from silence into sound without effort, focussed, yet free, with sufficient energy to release, or restrain, back of it, you are one of the greatest singers.

It matters not whether your voice be phenomenal or even beautiful, if it expresses the music and the words you will have an interested audience.

The largeness of that audience depends upon the quantity of personality you are able to put into your performance.

If you are magnetic, the world is yours.

If you will get the violence out of your diction without destroying the clarity of your enunciation, you may eliminate the roughness of your voice without weakening its intensity.

To sing well you must continually feel "hollow-headed," "full-throated," "broad-chested" and "tight-waisted."

Do not "hold" your tone, spin it. Hold your breath.

No matter what the character of the voice be (bass, tenor, contralto, soprano) it should feel high placed and sound high focussed.

Using low resonance alone has ruined every voice that tried it.

Relaxing a muscle is beneficial only to educate and discipline outermost muscles to do their part in a process.

Otherwise it is weakening to the final out-put.

It is co-action, not non-action, that causes controlled effort to feel effortless.

Lamperti never intended his pupils to relax while singing or breathing, but to accumulate the outermost energy and then to release it, as demanded by word and tone.

THE SECRET OF SINGING

THERE are three sensibilities that govern singing.

Sensibility to pitch and tone (over-tones) developed and controlled through nerves of hearing.

Sensibility to vibration and resonance developed and controlled through nerves of touch.

Sensibility to energy and breathing developed and controlled through nerves of entire body.

These sensibilities, though studied and developed separately, must be co-ordinated, so as to cause unity of action.

Unity of action of the three sensibilities takes place when imagination and emotion lead and command a performance.

Genius depends on his nerves of hearing and seldom realizes his full powers of touch.

Talent uses both sense of hearing and that of touch, and often excels genius.

The rest of us must acquire sensibility to the three, pitch, vibration and energy, and co-ordinate them, to compete with genius or talent.

Arousing and maintaining a continuous activity of this co-ordinated trinity of sensibilities, is the secret of singing.

Until you feel the permanency of your vibration you cannot play on your resonance.

Until you feel the resiliency and elasticity of your resonance you cannot modulate your voice.

Your tone must be part of the vitality of your body.

There are no muscle drones. All work as soon as a motive stimulates them.

What is co-ordination?

"All for each—each for all."

If any part of you pushes or pulls too much this fellowship of muscles and nerves is imperiled.

What brings success?

Vision, initiative and perseverance.

Let the desire to sing command your energies.

Let your singing educate and discipline your muscles.

Consider all else but gymnastics—setting up exercises.

KNOW THYSELF

OU gain nothing by imitating another.

Your physical machinery will finally rebell against a foreign idea.

A slow gradual growth—an evolution—is the only safe way to advance.

Every desire, every thought, every act must be an upgrowth from preceding ones.

A "grafted on" habit results in an impotent desire, a vain thought, a powerless act.

Your conscious act must result from your instinctive "urge."

"Know thyself" applies to singer more than to other professions, because to sing well, body, soul and mind are tuned together to do it.

The only things you can learn from others are to breathe slowly, and deeply, to pronounce correctly and distinctly, and to listen intensely and carefully.

The co-ordination and continuity of these three must come from yourself.

Know thyself.

A tone must start of its own volition, as a spark

springs to life when positive and negative currents meet.

Each muscle and every nerve must do its own work yet be bound to the will of the whole.

The feeling that your tone is free, borne on its own wings of energy, is one of the greatest delights of life—because you are its creator.

WHAT VOICE HAVE YOU?

YOUR voice has a way and a will of its own.

Do not prevent either, though you may direct the first and curb the latter.

The throaty voice must be left so.

The white voice has its right of way.

The dark voice must not be changed.

Some voices sound like flutes, others are "stringy" like violins, many are coarse and "reedy" like clarionets.

The low voice must not be pushed above its limit.

The high voice must not be pulled below its range.

The small voice should not be forced.

The large voice should have its fling.

Some voices are steady, others are tremulous.

The only voice that dare not be permitted to have its will and its way, is the breathy, non-supported voice.

"Why can't I sing?"

Because you try. Do you make an effort to speak? Well, the same process, a thousand-fold intensified and refined is the source of song.

When you can prevent movements without inhibiting reactions, you are ready to sing.

When your tone issues from the focus of vibration you are singing.

SINGING BY REFLEX

ON'T sing until you'd die if you didn't," said Lamperti.

There is a relationship, psychological and physiological, between the desire to sing and the body, similar to that between the necessity to sneeze and the muscular system.

Not by movement but by sensation do you control the delivery of your song.

When you are sensitive enough this can happen.

Only through the sense of touch in the mucuous membrane lining nose, pharynx, mouth and throat, does the mind control the vibration of the singing voice.

The network of nerves in this "inside skin" are connected with the brain. They keep the singer informed as to what is taking place in these cavities, and finally anticipate and control the vocal process.

Also, through the sense of touch in the tissues of the body does the mind control the power of the breath.

The myriad ganglia (nerve centres) distributed throughout the torso, though acting reflexively, telegraph to the brain all that is taking place in the muscles and lungs, and finally anticipate and control the action of breathing to sing.

Then the sense of hearing unites the pulsations in the voice and the energy in the breath to form the singing tone.

The nerves of the ear, whose tip-ends form the magical rods of Corti, keep the brain informed as to what this union of voice and breath is doing, and finally, anticipate and control the result.

Therefore the perfect voice is born of countless sensations. It is effective only when the utmost collective energy is controlled to produce it.

And when your emotional reactions to music and poetry are intense enough to arouse your entire personality, you are a great singer.

Should your singing become as reflexive and "unpreventable" as sneezing, you are one of the few lyric artists.

"How fast must I take in breath?"

If you do not dissipate the sensation in your head of the last tone, you can inhale as rapidly as you wish.

"Breathe through your tone," Lamperti said.

"Why?"

Because that is the position of singing. Why should you get out of position, while adding more energy to your breath power?

If you can not feel the focus of tone in the bony structure of your head, vibration is not intense and breath is not compressed.

What is co-ordination?

Freedom of action in every part, but with an understanding in every part of the mutual responsibility for the general result.

Until the energy in the vocal waves of vibration balances with the power in compressed breath, you have no control over your voice. Like two people trying to walk on the rails of a railroad—by holding hands they balance each other. They must be inseparable.

Skill is keeping flowing energy and uniform tones continually interdependent.

To do this everything must be so associated, that you can keep in mind what is past, be conscious of what is present and visualize everything in the future, in an orderly manner.

"Covered tone" is a misleading term. "Closed tone" should take its place.

In their inception all tones are dark to be opened or closed at will.

This muted beginning evolves into the "dark-light tone," which is the ideal quality of the human voice.

THE DARK-LIGHT TONE

LTHOUGH you may acquire a wide range of voice, you cannot modulate the sounds until the resonance of your tones becomes round and rich, *chiaroscuro.*

The pitch (vibration) of your voice seems to emanate from the back of the mouth (pharynx) spontaneously.

The resonance of your voice seems to originate in the front of your mouth (lips) voluntarily.

These two together seem to make the "dark-light" tone.

Though vibration alters its pitch it does not change its place (pharynx).

Though resonance has many colors it does not jump from place to place, but is modified by the movement of the lips in vowel formation.

The slightest escapement of compressed breath must arouse the pitch of the desired tone, vibrating intensely enough to be felt in the skull.

The continued escapement of compressed air should spin the tone to the required volume and color, filling the resonating chambers of head, mouth and (in low pitches) the chest.

The "dark-light" tone should be always present.

The weird feeling that the pitch of tone (focus of vibration) commandeers every thing beneath it, comes to the expert singer.

The chief thing that prevents this feeling is the muscular "attack" of tone, from beneath the focus.

Hearing in advance yourself singing the tone is the cause of this weird sensation.

When a tone begins loudly, the energy should come from the focus and not from the muscles beneath.

It is a release not a push. The tightened muscles in the torso loosen to permit this.

Your voice is focussed only when in its entire range it is intense enough to feel started and stopped in the same spot—the center of the skull.

VIBRATION, RESONANCE AND BI-NOISES

LWAYS remember that what "goes on" above the throat are illusions no matter how real they may feel and sound.

At the same time, observe that these illusions of the senses of touch and hearing are the only proofs that the throat is functioning normally and efficiently.

The more evident the sensation of resonance in the cavities of head and mouth, the better the "placement" of voice.

The more ringing the sound of vibration in the bones of head and mouth, the better the production of tone.

Both resonance and vibration must finally "take possession" of the cavities and bones of head, mouth (and in low tones the chest) and be permanently resident there.

Many times the bi-noises of the voice are inevitable.

Those caused by phlegm, emphasis, emotional effects, declamatory exclamations, aspirated emission, exaggerated pronunciation, etc., should not prevent the vibration and resonance of the voice from filling head and mouth and in low tones the chest.

Bi-noises do not "carry" and are unnoticed by an audience, if the succeeding resonance is rich and the following vibration ringing.

Vibration and resonance can cover a multitude of noises.

If preparing to sing does not straighten you up like a soldier, some essential part of your anatomy is not taking part.

While objectivity predominates, this feeling begins at the feet.

When subjectivity rules it commences in the head.

INNER AND OUTER MUSCLES

HE inner muscles of the larynx (those directly connected with the action of the vocal-cords) cannot function properly and freely in producing vibration and pitch of the voice, until the outer muscles of throat and neck are busy with pronunciation of word and resonance of tone.

In fact, these outside muscles are continually in a state of elastic tension (tonicity) in connection with the rest of the body.

The inside muscles attached to the vocal ligaments and cartilages of the throat (larynx) are tensed only while producing sound. They are not used during silences.

These inside muscles are compelled to do double duty if the outside muscles connecting head with torso do not know and perform their allotted work.

Of course these neck muscles are like-wise help-less, unless those of head and torso co-operate with them.

Only when the external muscular envelope of the whole body acts as a unit, can the internal muscles of the voice, untrammeled, function.

The diaphragm is also an inner muscle that can control breath, only when the abdominal and pelvic muscles co-operate with those of chest, neck and head.

The feeling of co-ordination from head to foot is that of being stretched in all directions at the same time.

Inner muscles act instinctively when outer muscles assist co-ordinately and continually.

HOW DO YOU BREATHE?

HY do you breathe?
            To purify the blood.
            How?

By drawing in oxygen to every cell of the lungs.

Well then do not insist that one portion alone should breathe to sing, or the blood returns to build up the body, still loaded with its impurities.

The precept "breathe low" means—control the breathing low in the body.

Feeling "hollow" in head, neck and chest—down to the waist—compels deep control of complete breathing.

"Satisfying" the lungs without dissipating the hollow feeling is the secret of song.

Not until the focus of voice is like a fixed star in your head, kept in position by the powers inside and outside your body, can you sing.

These powers are like gravitation, a balance of contending forces.

It is a mistake to breathe in just one part of the body.

Abdominal breathing alone brings high focused voice. But it remains throaty, small.

Diaphragmatic breath alone secures good diction. But resonance of head and chest will be lacking.

Intercostal breathing alone enlarges the low resonance. But diction will be faulty.

Clavicular breathing alone brings low resonance only. It destroys diction.

When the top and bottom of the lungs are equally full of compressed air, the voice will focus in the head, and awake all the resonance in head, mouth and chest. Diction then is master over all.

You must finally play on the rapid opening and closing of the glottis, not on the vocal-cords, as a violinist feels he plays on the vibration of the string, not on the string itself.

If singing does not feel like releasing energy to

sustain the voice, some important muscle is being held rigid.

The singing voice is so subtle and demands such multitudinous activities, that it can be controlled only when used naturally and thought about in a simple way.

Head, neck and torso form a drum like elastic unit, feeling hollow down to the waist, the rest of the body solid.

To maintain this condition without effort, singing or silent, is possible for every singer.

An effort or a movement must be a reaction in response to word or tone.

Rigidity or relaxation destroys the tonicity of this muscular unit, and imperils the control of the voice.

THE GLOTTIS MUST REMAIN INVIOLATE

WHAT the crystalline lens is to the eye, the glottis is to the voice.

The pulsating edges of the vocal-cords form the eliptical chink we call the glottis.

This chink opens and closes so rapidly that it produces what we call vibration-sound.

Though its action is instinctive, its functioning depends on what goes on above it (diction) and all the reactions beneath it (breathing).

Without compressed breath and distinct pronounciation it is useless.

Between this "above" and "below" must be a mutual understanding and working together to cause a balance between voice and energy as delicate as that of a chemist's scales.

Poor diction will disrupt this union.

Inadequate breath makes it impossible.

The moment violence or lethargy enters, the sound of the vibration changes from tone to noise.

This "entente cordiale" between word and breath, is stimulated and maintained, not by "method" nor "might," but by desire to please, and joy in performance.

The glottis must remain as inviolate as the quick of the eye.

The vocal cords, in separating, start the glottis to pulsating on the desired pitch.

The compressed breath then feeds this vibration with its inherent power.

The energy to start a tone must come from the

action of the vocal-cords themselves, as they separate, not from the impact of the breath pushed against them.

Then all tones spring from silence into sound without effort, making a *messa di voce*.

When you realize the facts, you must have enough common sense to readjust your singing to suit them, and cease your self deception.

If you are right, sensations and feelings will guide you.

If you are wrong, reason will right you.

There is no reciprocity between tone and breath, until the voice is straight, every vowel pure, and all consonants controlled.

Finally singing does not depend on voice and breath, but on a fusion of sound and air. This rids the voice of its "wolf-tones," *i.e.,* tones that have no harmonious overtones.

Noise is a naked skeleton.

Tone is fleshed in its own harmonics, and clothed in the overtones of surrounding space.

Release the compressed breath to start your tone, do not push nor pull muscularly.

The degree of loudness of tone depends on the quantity of breath released by "letting go" muscularly.

The gradation of this letting go is controlled by the diaphragm, which however is never relaxed.

FUSING VOICE AND BREATH

O not form permanent habits of singing until voice and breath are fused together, and all energies are co-ordinated.

When your singing voice becomes a reality it will use all the energies of your mind and body as easily as the speaking voice does.

The difference between speaking and singing is continuity of vibration and energy.

In speaking, momentum is constantly arrested; in singing, never.

Prepare to sing each succeeding phrase while still on the one preceding it. Do not wait until a word or melody ends, but gather your energies in advance. Then the taking of the breath does not break the continuity of the composition. Neither does diction interrupt the flow of tone, nor the readjusting for pitch and power endanger the vitality of the voice.

Your diction will be "mouthed" unless your voice is focussed.

Your focus will not stay "put" unless your words are on your lips.

Focus and diction are as reciprocal as diction and diaphragm.

In fact, diction, diaphragm and focus form an eternal triangle.

One cannot exist without the other two.

Pronunciation of words is controlled by sensations not efforts.

Focus of tone is purely a sensation, not an effort.

The diaphragm *re-acts* unconsciously to sensation of focus and diction.

The whole body reacts to keep this eternal triangle going.

Efforts annul the unconscious activities of singing.

It is foolish to think you can sing without arousing and controlling the acoustics of your head, throat and chest.

It is more foolish to try to do this with less than the entire energy of your mind and body.

It is gauging the release of this entire energy that makes singing easy.

An art intrigues your whole personality.

All processes seem reversed when your tone drives *you*.

Your voice begins first.   Your breath comes next. Your energy enters last.

VIBRATION

POWER either builds or destroys.

The energy in regular vibration is constructive.

The violence in irregular vibration is destructive.

Regular vibration causes the voice to be true to pitch, ringing in quality, and rich in character.

It demands compressed breath controlled by diction and diaphragm.

Irregular vibration causes the voice to be flat or sharp, breathy or pinched in quality and shaky in character.

It is the result of loose breath forced through the throat nullifying diction and diaphragmatic control.

There comes an added help in keeping the balanced union of voice and breath, similar to the help of resin on the bow.

Vibration of the voice is like the string.

Breath is like the bow.

What is this added help?

Regular vibration.

Like resin, it prevents slipping.

Energy can play on it, but not by push or pull.

Regular vibration excites the breath to feed it.

It is not heard by the audience.

But it is felt by the singer, in his head.

It is sometimes mistaken for hoarseness or phlegm.

When it appears in the voice it re-educates the entire process of singing because it becomes master.

It is this, that makes the voice feel like one register, one mechanism from top to bottom.

Excitation of muscular energy, not movement, prepares one to sing.

It prevents inhibitions.

Memory of how it feels makes your only method.

While the voice feels always focused in the same place, the focus has different degrees of energy, according to the energy of the breath power released to produce it.

The voice is a natural phenomenon of vibration, not an arbitrary thing.

It can be "turned on" or "off" at any time, like electric light.

To develop and control the "power" is the duty of a singer.

All the sounds of language and pitches of tone are the buttons.

The "carrying" power of the voice is equal to the inherent energy of your compressed breath.

The intensity of both vibration and breath is the same for soft as it is for loud tones.

For soft tones, though resonance is reduced and breath is held back, the voice remains vital.

For loud singing resonance is increased and more breath is released, without endangering the regularity of the vibration.

It takes more muscle to hold the breath energy back, than it does to let it go.

Therefore soft singing is more difficult than loud singing, and should be studied last.

Never use the voice without this carrying power.

The spinning vibration takes care of pitch and power.

The sound of the word controls resonance and color.

Co-ordinated breathing furnishes energy.

The two things to watch are focus of tone and control of breathing.

Diction is the offspring of these two.

Would you not be surprised to see a violinist hit the strings with his bow?

Well, do you wonder at the decline of the art of singing, when masters insist on their pupils attacking the voice?

All voices using the stroke of the glottis deteriorate rapidly. Natural singers are ruined thereby.

The voice is neither drum nor flute, but an instrument on which all the energies play. The power in the breath is the bow; your muscles but guide it. The abdomen is the hand, the diaphragm the fingers.

FAULTS AND STAND-STILLS

A PERFECT organ is rare.

The majority of throats and bodies are maladjusted. Some congenitally, others through injurious practices and bad habits of mind and body.

Most of us can be normalized.

All may be helped.

Psychological complexes are more difficult to overcome than physiological misfits are to readjust.

When both bodily and mental processes are wrong it is a long slow job to right them.

We should never be discouraged by failure, for it usually reveals a fault which may be corrected.

Nor need we be down-hearted over a "stand-still." It is nothing more than a warning that we have progressed too rapidly, and are "stale."

Courage overcomes a fault.

Patience cures a stand-still.

Faulty habits are usually the result of protective impulses.

In singing they are seldom corrected by stopping them.

The cause of a bad habit is generally found in some distant part of the body, which is shirking its duty, or acting antagonistically.

When that part of the body co-operates harmoniously with all other parts, the necessity of protection ceases, and the wrong habit disappears.

You can fathom most difficulties if you will reverse your thinking and acting. Nothing, then, escapes your notice.

Most failures are caused by confused thinking or acting.

Pulsation that becomes sound is as subtle as vibration that causes light.

Both are intangible.

Yet sound and light may be controlled.

All tones are "closed" until "opened."

When a tone "opens," the "focus" of vibration does not change.

Return to "closed" quality is impossible if the tone becomes too "white."

To bring word and tone to the lips, without losing the darker resonance is an absolute necessity.

To breathe without expanding the chest is an absolute necessity.

To keep the lungs full of compressed air, yet "satisfied," is an absolute necessity.

To continually feel the sensation of "hollowness" from head to waist is an absolute necessity.

To remain elastically "solid" from the waist to the pelvis, is an absolute necessity.

To maintain a tonicity of all muscles, without rigidity, is an absolute necessity.

When the voice is irresistibly attracted to the pitch of the next tone, you can sing.

Instinctively the body and mind react to this desire to attain and sustain the pitch.

When the voice is "in tune," it is "placed" and controllable by musical emotion, inherent in the desire to sing. Breathing is also actuated by this desire.

The habit of relying on local efforts is overcome only by the realization of co-ordination, and not by stopping said efforts.

When the texture of your elastic resonance seems part of your head, you are a great singer.

To anticipate the "feel" of resonance (vowels) before singing, and to keep the sensation during pauses and after singing, is the lost art of the Golden Age of Song.

To-day a singer seldom knows what effect he is going to make, and is usually sorry after he makes it.

Only when tone seems part of bone and muscle of the head, will energy flow from all parts of the body to produce compressed breath that feeds it.

It is well for a musician to recognize diatonic tones, and to know when these are chromatically altered.

This is absolutely necessary for singers.

The "movable do" is the surest way to arrive at this knowledge.

The feeling of perpendicular vibration from the focus in the middle of the skull to the pelvic control is a sign that the right and left vocal-cords and sides of the body are concertedly functioning, "synchronizing."

"CROOKED SINGING"

HEN both sides of the body act equally, instinctive singing is possible.

If this is accompanied by concerted action of both sides of the throat (synchronizing the efforts of the vocal-cords) spontaneous focus of tone is possible.

In fact, this balancing of the two sides is the chief result of objective exercises and study.

Very few voices have this perfect adjustment by nature, because generally the body is weak on one side. This side must be strengthened.

"One sided" singing is the chief cause of ugly and ruined voices.

If taken in time and the right exercises used, the voice will "straighten up."

Of course when caused by congenital deformation, the crooked tone must be permitted.

Though the start of a tone seems hum-like, and felt at a certain spot in the bony structure of the head, it is useless to insist on the sensation of a focus, until the body instinctively compresses and pelvicly controls breath.

The spot where tone seems to start, is the place where the vibration of "ng" (as pronounced in the word "*Eng*land") is located.

Because all tones high or low seem to start in the same place, the voice is said to have one register but three resonances.

Pitch of tones should be associated with harmonies and not with melodies:

Because harmonic sense is more basic than melodic sense.

Even in chromatic passages, the tones of the underlying harmony and not the "passing notes," keep the trueness of "tonality."

Intervals of whole and half steps are theoretical only, and on a keyed instrument, misleading.

The voice must be more in tune than the piano, which is "tempered"—that is to say, tampered with!

Singing is a subjective process.

Words and tones are born at the lips.

The reverberations of the room are but enlarged reproductions of the vibration and resonance in the head and chest.

Therefore you cannot sing until consonants and vowels emanating from the lips, set up voice sensations throughout skull and lungs.

Your artistry is as great as your diction and resultant voice sensations (inside of you) are distinct and efficient.

UN-SEEN, UN-FELT ENERGY OF THE VOICE

I T is the unseen and un-felt energy that does the singing.

This energy you accumulate before-hand and hold in check until it is drawn from you by word and tone.

It is an instinctive process.

Word and tone emerge from silence stealthily and steadily so as not to embarrass the regular flow of energy.

The starting and stopping of audible sound must be like the beginning and end of a thought, imperceptible, impalpable, yet vital. This is also instinctive.

The mucous membrane and bones of head, throat and chest, however, do feel the vibration of word and resonance of tone.

Finally it is the desire to experience these intense sensations of vibration and resonance of word and tone that causes the body to gather the un-seen and un-felt energy that produces them.

Never separate diction from singing, not even in thought.

Each word has its individual peculiarities.

Every tone has its special sensations.

These should be recognized and permitted.

Language and music must be studied until you realize the sound of words and pitch of tones.

The body must be developed and organized in order to produce the un-seen and un-felt energy that serves the sound of words and pitch of tones.

Find a symbol, an image or a thought that will lead and unify all efforts.

The idea that has helped me most, is that of continuity.

Every tone (loud or soft) must be vital and intense enough to "ignite" the next, notwithstanding pauses which may come between.

Another illusion is "my other self" (a sixth sense) that stands at a distance and tells me what, when and how to do.

It causes co-ordinate concentration of mind and co-operative action of body.

I seem to hear and see myself as others see and hear me.

Your voice will continue focussed in your skull so long as you sing with regular vibration in the throat, fed by compressed breath, controlled in the pelvis.

Your words and natural breathing organize your voice.

Your mental and physical gymnastics develop your energies.

Your musical and poetical imagination unite voice and energy and tunes and times your organ.

Your emotional nature plays on this sublimest of musical instruments.

"CHIAROSCURO"

HERE is vocal resonance like unto a composite vowel-sound containing all of them.

The reverberation of the voice is felt as an elastic solid filling head, throat and (in low tones) chest.

When this composite sound is focused in the middle of the skull, it can be moulded by the lips into any form or shaded to any color, changed from one vowel to another and made to open or close at will.

It is the "dark-light" tone, which unites all registers, that can be sung with mouth open or shut.

It demands control of all muscles from top of head to middle of waist.

Keeping such a tone focussed in the head depends on the connected energies from waist to pelvis.

In other words, you sing "from head to foot."

The vocal-bands then tune this "chiaroscuro" tone without push or pull.

When you can inhale without disturbing this ideal co-ordination, you are a great artist.

When heart and head unite, self-knowledge results.

Singing loudly is releasing; singing softly is restraining the pent-up energy in compressed air filling the lungs, co-ordinately gauged in doing so.

The greatest incentive to co-ordinate control is the insistant desire to do what you know perfectly well how to do with text, time and tune.

Behind your thought of word, rhythm and tone, back of your effort to consolidate your energies, lie your elemental powers.

Why not make use of them, organize them and let them lead instead of lag?

There is force in your primal nature like that which "moves mountains."

When this is tapped your voice attains a formative power of its own, independent of your body and mind, though served by both.

There streams from your mouth astonishing projections of resultant tones and harmonics, undreamed of before.

You must become familiar with the accoustics of your voice chambers and the room you sing in.

You must feel the sensation of actions and reactions that awake the accoustics of your voice chambers and the room you sing in.

Singing is possible only when you have brought it into connection with the current of your own experience and knowledge.

When you sing, mental and physical qualities are mixed together.

Organize your physical forces.

Systematize your mental processes.

Objective efficiency means mechanical impact.

To know the actual laws of singing is to control them.

When knowledge of singing is truly realized and vital, it carries the necessary action with it.

Singing is accomplished by opposing motions and the measured balance between them.

This causes the delusive appearance of rest and fixity—even of relaxation.

The singing voice in reality is born of the clash of opposing principals, the tension of conflicting forces, brought to an equilibrium.

"What is so foolish as to take unsure things for sure, and false things for true!" *Cicero.*

"It's what we learn after we think we know it all that counts," says Abe Martin.

Your elemental self remains aloof until you know text, tune and time. Then it takes command, is the real singer.

Of course it is necessary for breath to escape to feed pulsation of the glottis, as well as to "ease" the lungs.

If these collapse in so doing singing is ineffectual.

This happens when air is drawn loosely into the chest (instead of compressed) then pushed out to give it power to sustain the voice.

Escaping breath will turn to tone only when the inherent energy in the compressed air feeds the pulsations in the throat.

The lungs then never collapse, the voice never fails.

COMPRESSED BREATH

HE moment you have energy of breath sufficient for the phrase, re-adjustable for all details and all pitches in the phrase, yet continuous from start to finish, you can sing.

Loose, pushed out breath is useless even injurious, though you have lungs full, for it causes local efforts, irregular vibration and disrupted energies.

Compressed breath comes through co-ordination. It has only to be guided, and restrained. Its inherent power feeds all the effects made by the vocal-cords. It does not upset the pose of the voice. It permits the throat to act naturally, "open," as in talking. It does away with both breathy and pinched tones. It does not demand one quality of resonance only but commands all colors, from the darkest to the lightest and all pitches, from highest to lowest.

Compressed breath permits all effects made in declamation, provided same effects do not become a "method."

In fact, stereotyped singing is impossible, when breath is compressed. There is no "attack" no "mouth position," no "tongue control," no "voice placing," no "fixed chest," no relaxing this or that muscle, no stiffening any part of the body, in fact, nothing that would not spring from instinctive utterance.

Spontaneous speech or song seems to use only the air in the mouth for a start, after which the throat and whole body unite with the head to "keep things going."

Even then you seem to breathe only to satisfy the heart beat.

This you do as often as possible in a phrase, in little sips (thimbles-full), without arresting any action but the vibration of the vocal-cords.

The focussed start of all tones must be so powerfully charged with energy that it needs a guiding, restraining "hand" (diaphragm).

Only when this self acting "attack" is full of controlled energy can it be felt in the skull.

Of course this energy in the voice is dependent on the energy in the breath, not on the action of the throat.   The latter simply "tunes" the sound.

There is a great temptation to help "tune" the voice by either push of breath or pull of tone.
Both are full of violence, until a balance is struck.
Then the "tuning" in the throat is unhampered.

If the "tuning" of the voice is unskillful from lack of "ear-training" and knowledge of music, singing is a farce.

It is a strange fact that the throat is controlled by what happens above it, in the accoustics of the head, through word, vibration and resonance.
And stranger still is the realization that the lungs are dominated by the muscular system below them, in waist, abdomen, and pelvis.
Head and pelvis are mysteriously connected by co-ordination of all activities that lie between them.

When your voice comes out of your mouth as you expect and plan and at the same time you are obeying natural laws of vibration and breathing, you need have no fear of failure.

A flow of saliva is a sign of correct voice production.

A dry mouth and throat indicate wrong use of the voice.

The power to group words and phrases of a song together making one continuous whole stamps the real singer.

The common sense to link all activities of breathing and singing under one impulse, making a single operation, reveals the true artist.

You must catch the next tone mentally before the one you are singing stops spinning.

Mentally there is no silence, you are either singing a tone or spinning the interval between that and the next pitch.

This is the law of continuity of vibration and energy.

To obey this law, the body and mind are constantly in motion, with very little movement.

It is like the action of balancing on a tight-rope.

"ATTACK"

THE beginning of a tone (mis-called "attack") can be practiced only when vibration starts focussed in the centre of the skull (sphenoidal sinus) without effort or muscular impulse.

It is a "free-ing" and not a "hitting" process. The tone seems to come out of the head, instead of the throat.

The "dark-light" tone demands *this central start*.

It has all degrees of emphasis according to the

energy of compressed breath released to produce it. This cushion of breath must never be exhausted, but renewed at every opportunity.

When this beginning of vibration is inherent in the singer's head, each higher tone is drawn to its pitch, without muscular push, yet with adequate energy: each lower tone finds its pitch without relaxing energy, keeping the intensity of the higher tones.

Intense vibration only will awake this sphenoidal focus.

Resonance is but the streaming of these vibrations from the focus toward lips, throat and chest—according to the registers of the voice.

Your art is the fulfillment of your elemental desire to sing.

Your growth is stimulated by what you hear and understand.

If you faithfully do your daily practice, without anxiety about the result, you will find yourself competent in the end.

You must stop at no stage of progress, anchor to no habit, be satisfied with no result, exult in no success.

All the details of singing are finally marshalled under one commander, emotion, the original source of song.

FOCUS

OCUS of the voice is but the absence of irregular vibration and violent energies.

It depends on the "start" of tone, produced by a release of pent-up breath power.

It is "felt" in the head, though caused in the throat.

It is developed through use, and refinement, of vibrating consonants.

It is destroyed by non-vibrating consonants, if a focussed vowel does not follow these sounds.

A focussed vowel is the most difficult to control:

Because it must start like a needle puncture, expand into full resonance and disappear into silence, without undue effort, and no escape of air, other than to feed the vibration.

If the vocal-cords "hit" together to make an "attack" it is hurtful.

Focus of voice is started by these "vocal lips" separating.

They "smack" instead of "whack."

The focus of tone is like the converging rays of the burning lense. So intense is this "point" that it is felt wherever it reaches.

The glottis is the "lense."

Compressed breath-energy is the "sun."

Either relaxation or rigidity will destroy the focussing power of the glottis.

Loose breath will furnish no rays of vibration.

This sense of focus becomes the leading objective guide to the voice.

The desire to feel the "touch" of the "point" of tone, becomes the objective guide to the breath.

The consciousness of the focussing point of the voice in the middle of the skull becomes so permanent that it is always there, silent or singing.

Consciousness of focus needs no push nor pull.

Words are but dyes that tint the focussed vibration of the voice with their colors.

If "good diction" is an enemy to "good tone production," you are on the wrong road.

If pronouncing words "closes" the throat, blame the breath.

When you master releasing and restraining the breath to suit the sounds in words, the throat will never misbehave.

Progress is slow or fast according to the perception of the three fundamentals, pronunciation, vibration and breath energy, and the realization of the reactions that cause, co-ordinate and control them.

You will know when pronounciation is adequate by the feeling on the lips (almost a tickling).

You will recognize when vibration is controlled by the sensations in the skull (almost electrical).

You will feel when breath energy is serving powerfully by the excitation of the whole body (almost sensuous).

The health, normality, size and similarity of the ventricles (in the larynx) and their con-current action in voice production are of paramount importance to the singer.

A catarrhal condition, abnormality, diminutiveness, or unlikeness embarrass the singer, and lack of synchronization defeats all his efforts.

You must discover and learn how to excite the reactions in mind and body, that produce artistic singing, and know how to weave them into a performance.

You do this through knowledge of what is constructive, through realizations of the beautiful in music and poetry, and the desire to communicate this beauty to others.

You should be as unconscious of the start of your voice, as you are of the first movement of your train.

Both must be well conducted for this to be true.

The stopping of your voice (or a train) is also imperceptible, if well engineered.

There must be unlimited power behind your start (and after your stop) in your engine.

When you can start your voice with your mouth shut as well as you can with it open, you can sing.

When the voice retains the same hum-like sound and feeling after the lips part, as it has before they separate, you can sing.

When you can take your breath without dissipating the sensations of this adjustment (for the humming resonant voice) you can sing.

When you neither push nor pull, but let inherent energy in the voice and sensuous reactions in the body do the singing, you can sing.

SINUSES

THE various sinuses in head and cheek-bones, "shed" vibration, if the initial tone (pulsation of the glottis) is intense enough to start them echoing.

You cannot blow your voice into these cavities, nor pull your tone from them.

The ringing in these chambers depends on the instinctiveness, purity and intensity of the initial tone in the throat, and not on your efforts to "place" the voice.

The vocal-cords are helpless without the power of compressed breath to feed their pulsation. Therefore the lungs should never collapse.

"VOICE-PLACING"

 "PLACED" voice is one that is felt in the mask of the face as well as high in the head, in the pharynx and deep in the throat and on low tones in the chest.

The same sensations of sound waves are felt while speaking, seldom on a sustained pitch, more often rising and falling, "inflected."

Memory of these "placement" sensations in the head, nose, mouth, throat and chest is the controlling medium.

Natural singers have no trouble in maintaining the "posed" voice, because the whole body instinctively responds, re-acts to make it possible.

The rest of us through sensatizing gymnastics acquire both production and co-ordination often more proficient than in the "natural singer."

The term "voice placing" is a misnomer.

"Voice-finding" is a more appropriate expression.

Although the resonance in head, mouth and chest, and the ringing of the cavities in the bones of the skull, constitute the beauty of the voice, they are but the flowering of the germ-tone in the throat.

If this initial vibration is produced instinctively, as in speaking, yet with greater intensity (made possible by compressed breathing) the beauty of the resonant singing voice is sure to appear.

The sensations of resonance and echoing in cavities of head, mouth and chest, are the only evidences of proper and efficient vibration in the throat, and adequate control of breath-energy.

The mouth of the singer finally feels that it controls all back of it, voice, breath and body.

Until co-ordination is felt at lips, finger-tips and toes, singing is uncertain.

The softest murmur at the lips should cause the turning on of this complete current of united energy of the body.

The loudest (or the highest) tone of your voice is produced like the softest murmur, but with the full steam of co-ordinated energy freely released.

To keep co-ordinated energy "going" while singing or silent, is the great secret of the successful artist. This cannot be taught. You must work and wait 'til you feel it at lips, finger tips and toes. Natural forces governed by immutable laws of tonal vibrations and physical functions, make this possible.

Method is a delusion and a snare.

Success brings stagnation and failure.

Singing is an adjustment between mind and movement.

Attainment is a never ending climb.

Attack of the voice is the first escape of compressed breath which starts the vocal-cords to vibrating, after which no air is allowed to come out that does not turn into tone, and no breath must enter the lungs that is not compressed. It therefore behooves one to develop and control one's breathing, otherwise muscle effort instead of the inherent energy in the lungs is used to produce the voice. A reciprocal reaction between singing and breathing is established, which relieves the singer from undue or local efforts. This leads to finding the voice continually in the "mask" as well as in the pharynx and head, producing the dark-light tone (chiaroscuro).

Breathe through your tone without constricting your throat.

Compress breath without rigidity.

Place voice without violence.

Energy of tone and energy of breath must balance.

Although the initial vibrations are in the throat the tone seems and feels in the head.

Continuity and co-ordination are not efforts but self controlling necessities.

Self producing tones have a slow start and stop, while an attacked sound must have a "kick-off" and a rigid ending.

Objectivity alone is unrestful, awkward and rigid.
It can be used only for gymnastics.
Led by subjectivity it becomes restful, graceful and elastic.

Both are needed for final performance.

Suppress displacements and distortions in the body. They prevent co-ordinated energy.

Imagination fore-shadows word, tune and rhythm.
Emotion shapes, shades and times text, tone and tempo.

Difficulties in singing come from three directions: uneducated hearing, undisciplined muscles and untrained breathing.

What a line is to the student painter, a melody is to the singing pupil.
What values are to the artist's picture, harmonies are to the singer's song.

BLOOM AND SONG

ROM the trunk descend the roots of the rose tree into the ground, while from the same stem the branches are lifted into the air, and bloom.

From the waist descend the roots of breath into the abdomen while from the same place the branches of breath rise upward, and sing.

Blossoms open to the sun.
Tones open to the air.

It takes time for a tree to grow and bloom.
It takes years for a voice to unfold and sing.

Blossoms seem self-unfolding.
Tones feel self-producing.

The desire to bloom makes the tree grow.
The desire to sing makes the body develop.

The tree must wait for bud and bloom.
The voice must wait for word and tone.

The vigor of the blossom comes from the vigor
of the tree.
The energy of the tone comes from the energy of
the body.

Laws of nature control the tree that blooms.
Laws of physiology control the body that sings.

The first tone of a song must commence like spon-
taneous combustion; not like striking a match.
Anticipation of the next tone is the flame that leaps
to ignite its pitch.
This makes sure the line of melody.
Then the voice rides on its own vibration.
The flame must have energy to burn to leap the
many intervals.
The energy to burn is furnished by compressed
breath co-ordinately managed.

As the iris adjusts itself to light vibrations, so the epiglottis moves to suit the vibrations of the voice.

This cartilageneous muscle is raised to open a tone, lowered to close a sound.

(The epiglottis is the door to your "Sunday throat").

If your song does not "take possession of you," before you start, you are subjectively not ready to sing it.

If your song does not go easier and easier as you advance, you are objectively not capable of singing it.

Cell intelligence (sensation in nerve and muscle throughout the body) and atomic power (reactions that pervade the whole body and produce co-ordinated energy) are the two main factors in singing.

All else is "gymnasticating."

A song must gather intensity of emotion and energy as you advance from word to word and phrase to phrase.

It must excite a higher quality of voice and a lower control of breath with each succeeding syllable.

The last word of a phrase must find you stronger than the first.

Though the song come to an end, the sensations and re-actions continue 'til the curtain falls and the audience has gone.

It is the inherent quality of your tone (not your sputterings, gaspings, hiccoughings, gruntings, wheezings, rattlings, smearings, tremblings, scoopings, slidings, sobbings, cacklings, raspings, bellowings, etc.) that makes the beauty of your song.

You cannot be sure of the effect you intend to produce until you are conscious of the reactions that prepare you to make it.

Therefore the necessity of team-work of your subjective and objective powers.

A "natural voice" indicates a "good ear for music," a well poised and advantageously adjusted throat and body, adequate lung capacity, and an insistant desire to sing.

You know how the throat is behaving only by the distinctness of diction, the intensity of vibration, resonance of words, the volume of tone, and the ease in singing.

The desire to realize all these, and the effort to control them, trains the breath and the energies of the entire personality. The throat finally feels "open," as when speaking.

A constant bouyancy in head, neck and upper chest is essential to free tone production and good diction.

Some have called this a "fixed high chest," which is a misnomer.

There is nothing muscular about it, and it is not stationary.

It results from a desire to pronounce well and to give volume to the voice.

It causes no displacement in the body.

THE MAKING OF A SINGING ARTIST

HEN beginning a tone depends on releasing co-ordinated energy to start vibration of the vocal-cords instead of pushing breath to make a glottic stroke, you can sing.

When prolonging a tone depends on further release of co-ordinated energy to sustain the vibration of the vocal-cords, instead of pressing residual breath against a muscularly rebellious throat, you can sing.

When stopping a tone depends on cessation of vibration of the vocal-cords, without abandoning co-ordinated muscular tonicity, you can sing.

When vibration of the vocal-cords ignites the full resonance in head, mouth and chest without distortion and mouthing, you can sing.

It is ridiculous, foolish and injurious for you to make a ventriloqual effect, an imitation of your own or another's voice. There must be an instinctive, complete, co-ordinated re-action throughout the body.

If this does not happen, the throat is compelled to over-work to make up for this lack of assistance, and in consequence is unable to take care of its own duties—to furnish vibration and pitch of the voice and to help in pronunciation.

To start, sustain and stop word and tone, energy should stream toward the voice, not only from the lungs, but from every direction and all parts of the body.

Then, when from your softest to your loudest tone you control all the degrees of energy in your voice and body, you are a great singer.

This control of energy depends upon compressed breath and focussed tone, attainable through proper gymnastics in breathing and diligent exercises for the voice.

When from your most open to your most closed tone you control all the shadings of your voice, you are a great artist.

This control of color depends upon pronunciation of words, and completeness of resonance, accomplished through the study of language and practice of good diction.

When you control both energy of voice and color of resonance you are one of the greatest singing artists.

This depends on sensibility of the imagination and intensity of emotion and self-starting, self-sustaining and self-stopping tones. It is realized through poetical and musical stimulation and understanding, and balance between power of breath and energy of vibration.

It is a long road. But it pays.

There is a sensuous thrill in controlling the voice in song that is indescribable.

There is a spiritual joy in the artistic rendering of a song that is incomparable.

An artist is one who has met all the requirements, both objective and subjective, of his art.

Talent, though necessary, is not a substitute for knowledge.

Facility is advantageous, but cannot take the place of co-ordinated technic.

Emotion unifies, but needs imagination to arrange details.

Energy must not become effort.

The ideal tone, is a mouthful of sound that "spins," remoulds itself for every vowel, is felt at the lips, in the head, presses down the tongue, pushes up the vulva, even descends into the chest, in fact fills every nook and cranny.

Subjectivity alone leads to bigoted ignorance.

Objectivity alone produces organized stupidity.

Sub-consciousness and consciousness are the two ends of the same thing. Join them. Make them one.

Ignorance can be conquered by education, stupidity by unfoldment.

The great personality is one who acts intuitively, but shapes his act by thought.

Education should discipline, but not stifle subjectivity.

SUBCONSCIOUS POWER

URING the objective period of study the vocal-cords must be held together so that no breath escapes except that which becomes tone. It is a muscular process, which necessitates a conscious start.

When the subjective takes command, the vocal-cords (both false and true) are prevented from separating by the filling of the ventricular pouches with sympathetic vibration. It is a valvular, pneumatic process, which is self starting, self sustaining and self stopping.

The ventricles refuse to inflate, as long as breath is pushed through the throat, although the glottis may be induced to pulsate.

When inherent energy in compressed breath starts vibration of the vocal-cords, the ventricles instinctively fill with tone, pressing the vocal lips together, relieving them of all effort of approachment.

Any conscious effort produces irregular vibration, be it in pronouncing consonants, or vowels. This can not be helped. But it must not become a habit.

The voice is out of tune either in pitch or overtones (quality) until the subjective powers take command. Only then dare habits be formed.

Therefore your art is as great as your subconscious power.

Disjointedness in thought or action is the great mistake of art—even of life.

IMPORTANCE OF CONSONANTS

HERE are two natural falts to be over-come, rigidity and its opposite laxity, of the throat and diaphragm.

When the "pinchiness" of vibrating consonants, and the "breathiness" of those that do not vibrate, disappear, vowels begin to form spontaneously.

This is brought about by the reciprocal action of throat and diaphragm which excites co-operation of the entire being, body and mind.

The "start" of vibrating consonants (m, n, l, b, d, etc.), leads to a spontaneous start of vowels—and complete control of the throat.

The use of non-sounding consonants (s, t, f, p, k, etc.), leads to functioning of the parts that produce these noises, and management of the diaphragm (breath).

A forced development of vowels before consonants prevents good diction and endangers complete control of the singing tone.

Thus consonants and their refinements are of primary importance.

To cure the "nasality" of the consonant "m," cross it with "b," as if you had a "cold in the head."

The guttural quality of "b" disappears when combined with "m." It then vibrates more on the lips.

Think "d" while pronouncing "n," and the "twang" disappears, also like one with a "cold."

The "hardness" of "d" melts if buckled with "n." The noise seems then to come from the tip of the tongue.

The tightness of "ng" is lessened when united to "ig"—Again as with a "stopped up head."

"Ig" ceases to be unpleasant if softened by "ing." The sound then appears to start in the head.

Use these "cures" "homeopathetically," or they will do more harm than good.

Good singing demands the elimination of unnatural local efforts without weakening the intensity of the voice.

The "noises" of consonants develop into the sounds of vowels, and they in turn evolve into regular vibration of pure tone.

Pure tone finally seems to depend on its own inherent energy for both strength and duration, because it commandeers one's entire nature.

When you realize that nothing leaves the throat, (which only sets up vibrations) you will stop pushing and pulling to make your voice "carry." The "carrying power" depends on the regularity and intensity of the vibrations, and not on your efforts.

You cannot teach a muscle to act, but you can excite it to do so.

Learning how to arouse muscular action is the chief study in singing, not trying to "produce" and "place" tones, which are purely natural phenomena.

You *can* teach muscles to co-ordinate their activity and to prepare to serve the natural voice.

Efforts to sing are futile unless the two sides of the body "synchronize."

"Do the truth you know, and you shall learn the truth you need to know," has been wisely said.

The singing voice is a "castle in the air."

Imagination is its architect.

Nerves carry out the plans.

Muscles are the laborers.

The soul inhabits it.

Finally the desire to sing takes care of the full breath, and articulation of syllables, the half breaths ("thimbles full").

Though the voice starts like a spark, it has the potentiality of your entire energy.

The spark is the nucleus of your tone.

The abdomen is the base of your strength.

Every syllable you utter ignites the spark.

The diaphragm is the arbiter between tone and energy.

The mysterious moment when energy becomes life is beyond comprehension.

The magical moment when vibration becomes tone is equally baffling.

But creation takes place.

Phonation happens.

You can sing when in the roots of your being *you know you can.*

Your imagination moulds your song.

Your emotion colors it.

Your words clothe it.   It lives, moves, and has its being.

Your tone is true to pitch (in quality) only when the 5th or the octave is sounding with it.

The octave predominates in an open tone (vowel ah, eh, aw).

The 5th is more prominent in a closed tone (vowel ee, oo, oh).

MUSCLES

ALL muscles from the waist up must busy themselves with resonance and not with vibration. The lips through vowels chiefly control resonance.

All muscles from the waist downward control start, stop and intensity of vibration. The pelvis is the base of this control.

Pitch of tone is decided and controlled in the throat, independent of conscious muscular exertion. The vocal-cords do it. The musical imagination controls it.

Focus of tone consciously starts and remains in the bony structure of the skull. The sense of touch realizes it.

The lungs are only cushions of compressed air around which the body tightens. Co-ordinated muscles instinctively release this imprisoned energy as the voice requires it.

A stereotyped manner of inhaling defeats the singer. Each phrase must "take its own breath."

A conscious "placing" of the tone hampers the voice. Each utterance must "find its own place."

Trueness of pitch is but the working of the law of regular vibration, not a muscular process.

It is controlled in the pelvis.

Resonance is but the working of the law of radiation, not a physical effort.

It is controlled at the lips.

Tone and breath "balance" only when harmonic overtones appear in the voice, and not by muscular effort and "voice placing."

Then the tone can be modulated by every impulse of controlled breath.

A "focus" is the spot in the skull where the concentered rays of vibration (made in the throat) impinge.

"Focus" and pitch of tone, tho' produced and controlled by the body finally seem independent of it.

From the firmly attached focus hang the rays of vibration which weave the walls of resonance.

From the pelvic hand rises energy which grasps the feet of this bubble-like tone, making it alive, real.

Let the focus keep hold of the voice on a descending passage, as you would a "high strung" horse.

Let the focus draw the voice upward on an ascending phrase, like a babe at its mother's breast.

A sustained tone uses both reactions, equally, to "spin" its vibration.

A trill feels like twin-planets sustained in space.

The function of the throat is to spin vibration, not to hold the tone.

Vibration "taps" the energy accumulated by compressed breathing, and tone is the result.

The body releases this energy for loud singing and holds it back for soft.

Reposeful action brings economy of movement, making controlled mechanism possible.

Unity is maintained by linked action of all parts.

Over-action of one member endangers co-operation.

Non-action of any part breaks a link, and disrupts co-ordination.

TICKLE OF TONE

IF the sensations (tickle) of the resonance against the mucuous membrane of nose, pharynx and mouth disappear the mutual relations between voice and breath are broken.

These sensations must last from syllable to syllable, word to word and even phrase to phrase.

In fact, they seem to be ever present.

This is "voice placing."

If they predominate in the back part of the mouth and throat, hold the "cupped" hand over nose and mouth and feel the "tickle" on the palm of the hand as well as at bridge of nose, and in roof of mouth. This intensifies "singing in the mask."

The voice is an illusion of the two senses, touch and hearing.

Tickle of tonal vibrations and sensations of muscular energies unite only when emotion controls.

When these illusions and energies are continuous and intense, you are a great artist.

The ear is true only through team-work of thought and imagination.

Objective study is by thought through imagination to emotion.

Subjective control reverses this, when emotion arouses imagination which uses thought.

Until there is "consanguinity" in consonants you cannot sing.

Until there is relationship between vowels you cannot sing.

Until the mathematical accordance of two or more tones obtains you are singing falsely.

Pure tone is a "magic carpet" that lifts us and carries us through the realm of sound.

The throat does not furnish the power of the voice, it only decides the pitch and quality of the tone.

The diaphragm does not furnish the energy to sing, it only controls the use of the same.

Throat and diaphragm are inseparable in their action, and silent or singing are always functioning—never relaxed, nor ever rigid.

Imagination cannot pilot a shaky, leaky, lop-sided voice.

The voice must "find itself" ere the subconscious powers take possession and guide.

Emotion without a floating tone, wrecks the voice.

Only a full rigged voice can exist on the sea of sound.

OBJECTIVE

OU expect and get illumination when you start a light.

You expect and accomplish resonance when you start vibration.

The power of a light comes from the source of its energy.

The intensity of vibration depends on the strength that produces it.

Both the flame and the tone are natural phenomena.

Energy and strength to produce and control them must be striven for.

Get energy to burn.

Get strength that lasts.

The desire to sing should straighten you up like a soldier.

The tone you want to sing has a drawing power equal to the restraining of your energy.

You release energy only as the voice demands it.

The sensation of resonance is ever present in the head.

Vibration is "turned on" or "off" in this resonance: breathe through it.

"SELF-CONTROL" OF TONE

NTIL control seems to come from the tone-end of singing, you are only making noises.

To cause this to come true, you must mentally anticipate pitch, quantity and quality of every tone you sing.

Even then you are helpless, unless each tone arouses the right reactions in mind and body.

To make the body and mind efficient to serve the emotion to sing should be your chief study.

Tones "place" themselves, when your whole nature responds.

Violinists, 'cellists, et al., know and obey this law governing reactions to desire.

The voice (greatest of musical instruments) is absurd, without this "self-control."

AN "ARTIST"

OW foolish to think that such a phenomenon as vibration could be produced and controlled by mind and muscle.

They are only emotion's tools, which reproduce the sound the imagination hears.

Mind and muscle must be developed and sensitized to the "nth" degree, but they should never take command of the performance.

When the singer uses his intelligence and emotion on a 50-50 basis, he is an artist.

His success is as great as his personality.

Personality is a mixture of natural endowment, environmental influences and education.

This mixture of inherent qualities taps an elemental force which makes a genius.

Talent without education is helpless.

Education without talent is useless.

You do not accept a violinist who plays continually out of tune.

Why then applaud a singer who is off the key both in pitch and quality?

Virtuosity consists in seeing, hearing in advance everything that we perform with ease.

When we "materialize" what our emotion desires and our imagination depicts we are very great artists.

As a blossom draws strength to bloom from the plant, so the voice draws energy to sing from the body.

The larynx moves up and down to assist in modifying resonance (vowels) and not to aid vibration (pitch of tone).

Its position is governed by word and not by melody.

It is not the tone you hold, but the tone that holds you that is worth listening to.

It is not the air you take, but the air that the lungs want, that does the singing.

It is not difficult to sustain a tone.

It is not difficult to sing from one tone to another, if there is a common quality of vibration in the two tones, tho' the resonance changes.

Resonance is always changing.

Vibration, never.

The pitch of the voice is a subjective proposition.

The intensity of a tone is conceived by the imagination.

The quality of a tone is controlled by the emotion.

As long as there is objectivity alone the "hands" of co-ordination press against each other toward a centre, to keep from unlinking energies.

When subjectivity sets in, the linking is preserved magnetically (automatically) and the "hands" may press or pull as the "balance" of tone and breath demands. The prevailing sensation, however, is one of pulling (without breaking a link) in order to prevent "crushing" regular vibration of the vocal-cords.

When your high tones are not "pinched" and your low tones are not "breathy" you can sing.

High tones expand as to resonance, but do not spread as to vibration.

Low tones narrow resonance and broaden vibration.

Singing from the throat to the lips is easy, but inefficient, and precludes high tones. The voice remains too "white."

Singing from the head and throat simultaneously toward the lips, brings efficiency, producing a "darklight" tone that can be made somber or gay at will. High and low tones are then equally easy.

When the throat does not "try" to "vocalize," and the lungs make no "effort" to "breathe," you can sing, not before.

Develop local and general control, and wait for this miracle to happen.

Utilize your time studying piano and theory of music, and "reading" at sight.

Broaden your knowledge of literature, painting, etc.—the "beaux arts." This increases your "desire" for beauty, from which springs the instinct to sing.

When words, tones and breath conjointly produce your song, a remarkable leadership appears in diction.

Consonants and vowels start and spin tones with no effort other than that inherent in their own process of formation.

If one of the three (pronunciation, vibration, breathing) fail, the throat is over-taxed; it tightens and pitch of voice is disturbed.

When one of the trio (word, tone, breath) tries to dominate, the other two are rebellious, and rigidity of muscle endangers all three.

Each must be studied and analyzed separately, then practiced, exercised unitedly, before diction can take command.

Not until there is continued activity of this linked triumverate without jerk or jar will diction be able to interpret a song as the composer intended.

UNION OF WORD, TONE AND BREATH

EVER pull the voice away from its focus, nor push the breath up from its foundation, nor let diction leave the lips.

Never disassociate these three—word, tone, and breath.

The feeling of focus is like the touch of a feather within the head.

The sense of breath support is like the satisfaction of a good dinner in the stomach.

The sensation of good diction is like the tickle on the lips while "playing on a comb."

The union of this trinity is like three children playing in a ring, holding hands.

If one lets go, all are helpless.

Should any one become too energetic the others are embarrassed.

Word and breath are generally the guilty ones.

The vibration that comes from the focus always seems small.

The resonance that is started by the word usually feels large.

The energy that streams from the body appears inexhaustible.

When energy ceases, the union dissolves.

The throat feels "open" only when diction controls vibration, resonance and breath-energy as a unit.

Good diction alone excites the pneumatic action in the throat, causing it to feel "free," at the same time it commandeers the energies throughout the whole body and mind.

Then singing is easy, and a pleasure to both artist and audience.

Technique must touch the "quick" of your being.

The voice is pneumatic.

(Ventricular pouches in the larynx inflate when both false and true vocal bands (vocal-cords) approach and meet like two pairs of lips when kissing).

Ventricular action is as necessary to the singing voice as the pulsation of the glottis.

Therefore the voice needs both regular vibration, and full resonance before it can be controlled.

This is what a "natural singer" does.

The rest of us must learn to do it.

The hollow feeling in head, throat and chest is an indication of ventricular preparation to sing.

Why are the high tones of the majority of singers pinched and small?

Because the throat is made to do double duty—control the breath current and furnish pitch of vibration.

As the voice ascends to higher tones, control of breath should descend toward the pelvis.

On low tones this gauging is felt at the diaphragm, and even higher.

When breath is held and controlled abdominally (from waist to pelvis) the voice is free to expand on any tone high or low.

HIGH TONES

HERE must be enough controlled energy and momentum of vibration in a tone to send the voice from any pitch to tones higher than that pitch. The wider the skip the greater the power and intensity in the pulsations of the lower tone. At the same time the higher tone is more resonant than the lower.

The voice then seems to be "drawn" from pitch to pitch on an ascending passage.

This is the only way to produce high tones easily.

It is wise to practice descending scales and passages until this possibility arrives. Keep intensity and energy in the vibration, but reduce resonance as the voice descends.

Finally the height and depth of perpendicular vibration is the same for all tones. The voice changes only its resonance, thereby causing the so-called "registers."

When the whole range of your voice feels stationary and only resonance changes, you are a great singer.

When you breathe only to satisfy the demand for oxygen throughout the lungs, energetically, you are breathing as a singer.

Your singing tone seemes to start before you open your mouth and to remain after you close it, making a veritable "messa di voce."

This hum-like vibration continues from word to word and pitch to pitch, even leaps over silences.

It is dependent on abdominal control of breath and heady focus of voice.

This gives the sensation of perpendicular vibration (near or in the spinal column) from head to sacrum.

The bony structure of the body vibrates sympathetically with this hum-like perpendicular vibration.

There are two faults that dissipate the feeling of perpendicular vibration:—opening the mouth too much in forming vowels, and gutturally pronouncing consonants.

You must be conscious of this spontaneous sensation of hum-like tone before the curtain rises, and keep it until the audience has departed.

DON'T "HUM"!

WHEN Lamperti said "Singing is humming with the mouth open," he did not mean that humming with the mouth closed would bring this about.

"If you cannot sing with your mouth open, you can not with it closed," he would exclaim. "You cannot hum right, until you can sing right, although the mouth whether open or shut, feels sealed at all times."

The "hum" is the initial vibration, nothing else.

Controlled, it unifies the whole voice, equalizing all registers, head, medium and chest, eliminating "attack" and "breaks."

"The voice has one register, but three resonances," said Lamperti.

The "hum" in the voice is the unifying principal.

It is induced more by consonants than by vowels.

It is the rain-bow bridge connecting voice and breath.

Don't hum!

Failure to sing well comes from four sources:— loose breathing, mouthing words, spreading voice and disjointed muscular efforts.

Singing will be awkward unless focussed vibration, distinct pronunciation and compressed breathing remain inseparably linked together.

To retain the sensations, and continue the feeling of co-ordination of singing, without constricting the throat or stiffening the muscles of the body, marks the great singer.

Many confuse this ease of united action with relaxation, because laborious effort ceases.

When sensations of vibration and feeling of elastic muscles un-link, throat and body are forced into unnatural action.

SILENT BREATHING

INGERS who resort to loud breathing (constricting the throat and making an asthmatic sound while inhaling) do compel the body to compress the inspired air. This is fatiguing to the singer and unpleasant to the listener. Moreover it makes the throat do double duty, watch over both ingress and egress of the air.

The mouth and nostrils equally guard the entrance of air into the lungs. Even they should be noiseless in so doing.

Silent breathing should be the rule except for emotional effect.

If the singer wishes to secure diaphragmatic and abdominal control of his breath, he himself must not hear the inrush of the breath.

When silent breathing becomes "second nature," the singer finds that he never breathes hurriedly nor spasmodically, and always has plenty of air in the lungs.

Loud fast breathing sucks the air into the top part of the lungs only. The throat must control its exit.

Slow noiseless inhaling commences at the bottom and fills gradually toward the top, retaining the abdominal participation in the act. The diaphragm controls the exit of the breath to produce all sounds at all pitches.

The singer finally feels that he creates the energy to sing inside his body, as he does in speaking, all breathing being reactions to words and melody and emotional content.

From where does a singer get the enormous power he must use while singing?

From compressed breath, which is obtained by slowly and silently inhaling until the body is packed with air from pelvis to collar bone, with little or no expansion of the lungs.

The vocal-cords, with the help of the diaphragm, lips and uvula, use this dynamic air to make the sounds of words and sustain the vibration of tones.

In singing these, the throat, with little or no effort, has but to furnish the pitch and intensity of the voice.

The head when rightly poised reinforces the voice like an elastic loud-speaker.

The ease with which tones are started and sustained, and the distinctness of pronunciation of words, are marks of the singers control of his enormous power.

INCORPORATED BREATH

IT is useless to make an effort in one part of the body unless it stimulates correlated action in other sections.

This is especially true in the acts of inhaling and exhaling.

The whole torso as a unit contracts and expands, co-ordinately.

The shoulders and hips are linked together in preventing expansion while filling the lungs for the purpose of singing.

The pelvic region and breast bone mutually bear the strain of the energy in the inspired air.

The force of this compressed breath crowds upward toward the "wish bone" causing the singer to feel broad shouldered and high chested. (The breast bone is attached to each shoulder.)

There is no pressure of breath against the throat until the desire to speak or sing occurs.

Then the voice spontaneously begins to vibrate, the diaphragm permits enough breath energy to escape to produce and feed the pulsations that we call tone— and without push or pull of muscle.

The throat unembarrassed then functions in response to pitch and diction.

Incorporated breath is the most essential thing in singing.

When vibration of the voice is intense without being coarse (irregular) or throaty (vocal-cordy) artistic singing is possible and easy.

There must be this ringing quality (call it "overtone") in each sound you produce that "reaches" up or down and ignites the next word and tone.

True beauty of style demands that:—

Pronunciation should be energetic, but not exaggerated.

The audience should understand each word but not be conscious of your pronunciation.

Expression should be fitting, but not overdone.

The audience should feel with you the musical and emotional content of each sound you utter, without being conscious of your manner.

Every word and tone must have a reason back of it.

INTERPRETATION

THERE are three fundamental necessities in interpretation: adequate technique that serves; style that originates in the singer; emotional mood (depicted by composer and poet) in words and melody.

Unity of an interpretation (or creation) is dependent on the aural imagery of the song *as a whole*. Attention to detail belongs to the studio and not to the stage. The singer loses continuity of sensations and feelings the moment a detail obtrudes itself on his consciousness.

There is continuity of good tone as long as sensations of vibration (and resonance) and feeling of coordination (muscular activity) remain inseparably linked, silent or singing.

Memory of these sensations and feelings, and desire to experience them, prepare one to sing.

Realization of the interdependence of these sensations and feelings, is the acme of technique.

Interpretation is never twice alike. Accidents, mistakes, forgetfulness, fright, illness, exaggeration, etc., imperil the performance. Objective technique then prevents failure.

Interpretation also changes with every performance, if the singer is true to his musical and poetical emotion. Stereotyped style and expression prohibit this.

Your song is born of your imagination.

Your technique springs from your thoughts.

Your interpretation is moulded by your emotion which welds imagination and thought together.

DO NOT YAWN!

NE can not yawn unless one succumbs to the desire and feels the co-ordinate sensation.

One can not sing unless one feels the co-ordinate sensation, and succumbs to the desire.

The gratification of singing is more sensuous than that of yawning.

This "pleasure" continues throughout a song. The satisfaction of yawning soon passes.

However the sensation of singing and that of yawning are similar, in that both are all-stimulating, all-compelling, all-pervading.

But yawning does not help one to sing, though it may make one realize the sensation of co-ordinate reaction.

One can not yawn unless the desire is urgent.

"Do not sing unless you'd die if you didn't."

This was Lamperti's way of saying "Singing is like yawning," though he never intended one to yawn while singing.

Many have misunderstood and tried to do both at the same time, hoping thereby to superinduce the feeling of an "open throat."

Any arbitrary use of the throat, other than procuring a tone's pitch or a word's color, is detrimental to control of the voice.

Do not yawn.

PRESCIENCE

NTICIPATING mentally, sensing physically, feeling emotionally, poem and composition, makes a singer.

Hear your song in advance as though text and tune came from your own imagination.

Sense your voice before it starts, while it sounds, and after it stops, as though it were part of you.

Feel the mood of words and music as though they were to be your own emotional outpourings.

Hearing must be continuous.

Sensing must never stop.

Feeling must pervade all.

A FOCUSSED TONE

HAT is a focussed tone?

A self-starting, self-stopping sound.

What causes tone to focus?

Effortless, non-violent yet intense vibration of the vocal-cords.

What makes vibration of the vocal-cords intense?

Inherent energy in compressed breath which feeds it.

Why is vibration, though made in the throat, felt in the head?

Because there is no obstruction in its way 'til it strikes the bony element of the skull, directly above the throat.

Why does vibration always "hit" the same spot at the top of the pharynx?

Because there is an open path to that spot.

What helps me to "feel" the start of vibration at this post-nasal spot in the head?

The sympahetic reverberation of the middle sinus in the skull—an enclosed cavity in the head directly above the pharynx. In fact, the bony structure of the skull reports all that happens in the throat.

What can prevent the focus of tone?

Pushing non-compressed inhaled air toward the throat to start it.

How can I make a focussed tone?

You can't! It happens!

It happens when relationships between all parts of body and brain are established, completing the web of co-ordinate action.

What must I do to weave this web of united action?

Emotional imagination knits together all action. You can only give yourself up to it, and let it control you.

A focussed tone is like the rainbow—it "happens."

SOLFEGGI AND VOCALIZZI

IME and energy are wasted practicing solfeggi and vocalizzi, unless they have musical worth. Even then they must appeal to the needs and desires of the pupil.

It is better to sing simple songs and arias, using the movable DO. When pronunciation has improved enough to assist in tone production, these same compositions with their texts may be included in the repertoire.

Singing vowels on melodies (*vocalizzi*) is detrimental to progress, unless it can be done without undue throat effort.

"When one tone feels like another, you may vocalize. Until then sing syllables. Do, re, me, fa, sol, la, ti, do, are as good as any." (Lamperti).

Musicianship, as well as vocal technic, grows apace when the movable "do" is used.

Finally, musicianship should be far enough advanced to permit the student to invent, even extemporize, his own solfeggi and vocalizzi. This stimulates his musical imagination and emotional reaction, which are more important than mere vocal technic. Creative musical intelligence also develops thereby.

Fundamental exercises should be practiced daily, with syllables and when a student is ready, with vowels. But they ought to consist of simple scales and arpeggi especially adapted to the individual student, and his state of progress.

ESCAPING BREATH

IT is not breath, but pent-up pneumatic energy that feeds initial vibration of the singing tone.

To be able to accumulate this confined power and control its release, to feed the pulsation of the glottis, is an absolute necessity for every singer.

Escaping breath acts as an entering wedge "splitting" the vibration.

To counteract this, the singer muscularly tightens his throat, and guttural tones result.

"There are two ways of singing badly—breathily or gutturally." (Lamperti).

A focussed, dark-light tone is a sign of healthy relationship between initial vibration and compressed breath.

Such a tone can be "played on"—made loud, soft, dark, light, somber, gay—without disrupting the connection between vibration and breath.

The initial vibration must never be diluted with escaping, unvocalized breath, nor crushed with muscular effort to prevent the same.

DO NOT RELAX

THE "production" of the singing tone is dependent on the sustained intensity of initial vibration and the continuous release of inherent breath-energy.

Initial vibration must always be spontaneous and regular, yet dynamic.

Inherent breath-energy must be always ready and powerful, yet subservient.

Union of these ever present factors (not effort of the singer) "produces" the singing tone.

Because of co-ordinate action, which intrigues the whole personality, muscular effort and will-power seem in abeyance.

This gives rise to a feeling of ease—an equapoise— so insidious that a singer begins to rely on relaxation of mind and muscle—a quicksand that brings disaster.

Energy of brain and body must be cumulative, permitting the singer to end his phrase without calling on residual breath and reserve will-power

"You must be able to sing a phrase twice before you try to sing it once."

"Take breath as often as possible."

"The vibration of one tone ignites the next."

So spake Lamperti.

Do not become rigid!

But never relax.

THE SOUL OF A SINGER

THE soul of a singer demands technic of both voice and breath before it will emerge as tone.

Intense vibration and adequate energy must be ever available.

Overtones are its colors:

Rhythm is its heart-beat:

Resonance its body:

Vowels the·forms it assumes:

Consonants are its hands:

Emotion is its life blood:

Imagination its ears and eyes:

Thought its feet:

Desire its wings:

Melody is its language.

The soul of the singer is the subconscious self.

It can use the body and mind only after these are disciplined by the conscious self.

LAMPERTI AND HIS PUPILS *

IOVANNI BATTISTA LAMPERTI was born in Milan, Italy, 1839. His father was Francesco Lamperti. His mother's maiden name was Amalia Lupetini.

At six years of age he began the study of the piano with Dugani.

When nine years old he was first soprano in the Milan Cathedral, receiving 100 Austrian *lire* monthly. Bergamo was choirmaster. He kept this position two years.

At eleven he entered the Royal Conservatory of Music at Milan, studying piano with Angeleri, composition with Laoro Rossi, the director of the Institution. During this period he was playing accompaniments for his father's singing lessons.

At fourteen he left the conservatory, having completed his studies in composition and on the piano. His reputation as an accompanist was so great that the conservatory often sought him to play on special occasions.

Strange to say, his secret ambition was to be an actor. It was his father who insisted on his being a musician. His mother, brothers and sisters had absolutely no talent for music. He had a great passion for flowers.

* This biographical material, first published in *Singing and Playing Magazine*, is compiled from notes taken down by the author as Lamperti gave the data.

The great artists who made the most impression on him, and who in later years became his friends were Tomasso Salvini, the actor, and Cassola, the tragedienne, who was Salvini's first wife. Salvini in the drama "I Pagliacci" and Cassola as *Elizabeth* in the "Queen of England," interested him especially. The soprano, Fresolini (1852) in "Somnambula" and the tenor Negrini, a blacksmith, were his favorites. The latter sang only in Italy and Spain, fearing other countries would not appreciate him. His diction was marvelous. He had great admiration for and friendship with Landi, the tenor, and Giorgio Ronconi, the baritone. The latter was the first to sing in the registers of a baritone, as here-to-fore there had been only bass, bass-cantante and tenor.

The youthful Lamperti became so celebrated as an accompanist that the great singers came to him to coach in operas. All those years he was daily at the piano in his father's classes.

With these associations he was thoroughly formed as a master of the art of singing.

At the age of sixteen he announced himself, as *maestro di canto*, and soon had many private pupils.

His special preference was for the tenor voice, although he liked baritone and soprano. For the contralto, "a woman with a man's voice," he had a great antipathy. Nevertheless he was as successful in training them as he was with his favorites.

At this time, sixteen years, he wrote "Twelve Solfeggi" for soprano, mezzo-soprano and tenor.

At spare moments he was working on his opera "Cristoforo Columbo." In fact, he was undecided whether to devote his time to composition or to teaching singing.

In 1858 his pupils began to appear in opera. Antionetta Brambilla, made her début at Padua; the baritone Brunto at Milan; Mariani, the tenor, at Novara; Vidal at Como. The last named sang throughout Europe with great success and became a leading master of singing at Milan.

At this time he became very noted as *maestro concertatore*—that is, he drilled, directed and presented operas. His presentation of Rossini's "William Tell" (which had remained unheard for twenty years) was a special credit to him.

He now published his "Scuolo di Canto" for all voices, and "Twelve Vocalises" for soprano.

His pupil Hofrichter became prima donna in opera at Prague; Mecenseffy, the soprano, sang leading rôles at the Imperial opera in Vienna.

As *maestro concertatore* he gave "Moses," Rossini, and "Lucia," Donnizetti, at Bergamo with his pupils in the cast; among others, the basso Susini as "Moses."

The war with Austria now interrupted his professional activity. He became an officer in the army.

In 1861, on returning to his profession, he had among many other pupils Colonesi, the baritone and Morini, the tenor. These two singers were engaged at the Scala Theater at Milan, making their first appearance in "Lucrezia Borgia." They sang also in "Judith" (Peri) and "Faust." It was the first time Gounod's masterpiece was given in Italy in the Italian language.

Some of the directors of the Scala objected to Morini's enunciation. But Lamperti devoted all his time to the rehearsals, with the result that Morini surpassed himself.

On the afternoon before the evening performance, as he came into his father's studio, the latter jumped up from the piano and exclaimed before all the pupils, "You stay down there bothering with those chorus singers and leave me here to do all the work!" (It was not the first time his father had shown jealousy). The son turned and without a word left the house. The relationship of years was broken forever.

Up to this time father and son had been so closely associated that they were like one person, both teaching in the same home.

He now left his home and established himself alone.

However, in the same year, the elder Lamperti falling ill, the son took entire charge of the father's private pupils, and, at the request of the director of the conservatory, taught all the Lamperti classes in that institution.

From now on he had phenomenal success, many of his parent's pupils coming to him for instruction.

In 1863 his pupil Roberto Stagno made his début at Genoa in Flotow's "Stradella." He soon became one of the world's greatest tenors, singing in all the cities of Europe and America, for more than thirty-five years.

In 1864 Paolo Polilenzi made his début in "La Juive" at Como.

Vidal as *Faust* and Polilenzi as *Mephisto* sang in Como. Vidal also appeared at the Scala in "Don Pasquale" and at the most important opera houses in Europe. He later became a noted professor of singing at Milan.

Rosa Babette Castigilione made her début at Bari and later taught singing in Milan.

Guiseppe Francelli, tenor, after making his début in "Sonnambula" was chosen by Verdi to create the role of "Radames" in "Aida" at the Scala.

In 1865 Emma Howson appeared in "Dinorah," and later taught singing in New York.

Montobri, Hypolite Bremon, Sofia De Monteglio, La Chiomi, who sang with Strachosch in London and Paris, and many others, appeared at this time.

In 1870, Lamperti received a diploma from the Milan Royal Conservatory as to his ability to teach the art of singing, also stating the fact that he taught his father's classes in that institution, and mentioning his studies as composer and pianist as well as his compositions.

His pupil, Amalia Fossa, made her début at Bucharest in 1871, singing for many years at Madrid, St. Petersburg, Lisbon and Paris. She was chosen by Verdi to sing in "Forza del Destino."

It was through La Borgdani, a pupil, and her mother that Marcella Sembrich came to study with him.

A pupil, Stanslavo Mireski, became professor of singing at Warsaw.

Gottschalk taught in Chicago.

In 1876 Lamperti received the title of Chevalier of the Order of Charles Third.

In this year Paolina Marinelli and the tenor Bardi made débuts in "Don Sebastino" at Carcamo Theatre, Milan.

Charles Adams made his début at the Scala in "L'Africaine," later becoming a celebrated teacher in Boston.

Mme. Harris-Zaguri appeared at Carcamo Theatre in "Lucia," at the Scala in "Puritani," and later sang at Covent Garden, London.

In 1875 Ravizza (*soprano legero*) sang in opera at Milan, Berlin and other cities.

Helene Hastreiter made her début at Trieste in Verdi's "Don Carlos." She had a brilliant career in Europe and America. She revived "Orfeo" in which she had great success.

In 1876 Emma Wiziak sang at Caramo Theatre in "Ione" (Petrella), and later taught in Buenos Aires.

Maria Mark appeared in many operas.

Weiser (soprano) sang "Traviata" in which Nicolini (tenor) made his début. Nicolini married Adelina Patti.

In 1876 Lamperti was elected honorary member of the Royal Academy of St. Cecilia, Rome, as a master of composition. For the same merit, the Philharmonic Academy of Bologna, also made him an honorary member.

In the year 1878 his pupil Marcella Sembrich appeared at the Scala in airs from "I Puritani" and "Dinorah." She made her début in opera ("I Puritani") at Athens, Greece, in 1879, after which she was engaged at the Royal Opera in Dresden.

In 1879 Lamperti wrote "Preparatory vocalises" for all voices (Edition Ricordi).

This year, at the request of Mme. Sembrich, he removed to Dresden, where he established himself, many of his pupils following him thither.

In 1880 he wrote a concert aria with orchestra—"Bice"—for his talented pupil Sembrich, who sang it with the Philharmonic in Dresden.

In 1881 he wrote a "Marche Militaire" for orchestra, dedicated to the King of Spain (Edition Ries, Dresden).

This year Bertha Pearson was engaged at the Royal Opera in Berlin, where she sang for many years. She also appeared in Italy and America.

Syrwid, soprano, sang with the violinist Sarasate in Dresden, and later in opera at St. Petersburg.

Landi (tenor) concertized in various places, later appearing in opera in Spain and Italy.

In 1883, Horbowski became professor of singing at Warsaw.

Sleisiger, soprano, made her début in "Lucia" at the Rossini Theatre, Venice, and afterward sang at the Imperial Opera in Warsaw, where she also became a teacher.

D'Angeli became a concert singer.

Biron de Marion sang in opera in Germany.

In 1884 Agnes Huntington appeared in concert and opera in Europe and America.

Poly sang in concerts at Prague, in opera at Livorno.

Noejé was selected by Sir Arthur Sullivan to create the rôle of "Ivanhoe" at Covent Gardens, London.

In 1887 Lamperti wrote a brochure on the "Decadence of the Art of Singing.

In 1893 his pupil Daniel Griffith was selected by Anton Rubinstein to sing his songs in the Gewandhaus, Leipsig.

In 1905, he published "Technique de Bel Canto" in Germany and Austria.

He was unable to recall hundreds of his pupils, even many who became celebrated artists. Here are a few names he remembered I quote verbatim from the notes I took at the time: Charles Adams White, Boston; Louise Powel, Washington, D. C.; Popiquet and wife, Paris, France; Elsa Salvi, Dresden Opera; Paula Tullinger, Dresden Opera; Margaret Frazer, Pittsburgh, Pa.; Geiger, Indianapolis, Ind.; Brocket, Pittsburgh, Pa.; Hubbard, Chicago; Miss Williams, Chicago; Carrie Kidwell, Washington, D. C.; Vogt, New York; Ratcliff-Caperton, Philadelphia, Pa.; Frank Fair, Chicago; Janaret, London, England; Criticus, Paris, France; Saxhofmeister, Dresden and Berlin operas; Ziegler, Dresden Opera; May Stone, New York teacher, Zurich, Cassel, Berlin and Boston Opera Company.

In 1905 he removed his school to Berlin, his pupils following him. His class was so large that he secured his pupil, Wm. Earl Brown, as assistant.

Many singers had instruction from Lamperti: among others were Paul Buls (Dresden and Berlin operas), Carl Sommer (Dresden and Vienna operas), Schuman-Heinck and Edyth Walker.

LAMPERTI TO W. E. B.

"The mantle of my Father, Francesco Lamperti, fell upon me. It now descends to you, for you have grasped the truth of the Old Italian School of Singing, which descended from the Golden Age of Song, by word of mouth. It is not a method. There is no "bell canto" system of teaching. Mental, physical and emotional reactions are the fundamentals of this old school."

G. B. LAMPERTI TO WM. EARL BROWN.

ORIGINAL CERTIFICATE

Scuola di Canto
del
Cav. G. B. Lamperti
Gia
Professore di Canto
nei reali
Conservatori di Musica
di
Milano e Dresda
Socia Ordinario
della reale
Accademia di S. Cecilia
in Roma, etc.
Dresda, addi 9 Luglio, 1893

ATTESTATO
*Avendo il Sig. Wm. Earl
Brown, finito gli studi con
lodevole prova della sua va-
lentia nell' insegnamento
dell' arte del canto Italiano
sotto la mia direzione, ri-
lascio al medesimo la pre-
sente lettera patente dichia-
randolo abile insegnante di
detta arte.*
(Signed)
IL PROFESSOR
G. B. LAMPERTI.

(TRANSLATION)

School of Singing
of
Cavaliere G. B. Lamperti
former
Professor of Singing
in the Royal
Conservatories of Music
of
Milan and Dresden
Associate Ordinary
of the Royal
Academy of Saint Cecilia
in Rome
Dresden, July 9, 1893

ATTESTATO

Wm. Earl Brown having
finished his studies with
praiseworthy proof of his
talent for teaching the art
of *canto Italiana* under my
direction, I give him this
present letter patent de-
claring his ability to teach
said art.
(Signed)

IL PROFESSOR
G. B. LAMPERTI.

SUPPLEMENT

LAMPERTI NOTEBOOK

and

Selected essays from the

WM. EARL BROWN MANUSCRIPTS

edited by LILLIAN STRONGIN

LAMPERTI NOTEBOOK

The following is a record of Mr. Brown's lessons with Lamperti in Dresden, Germany, in the years 1891-1893. These notes, written in French, were dictated to Mr. Brown by Lamperti and are in Lamperti's exact words. I have endeavored to make a literal translation of these notes.

— — — —

Position — like a soldier.

How wide should the mouth be opened? — as wide as finger thickness.

Take a deep, full breath without retaining in lungs.

Take a deep, full breath, then let out very slowly.

Take a deep and full breath, condensed, then with tone let out only as necessary for the tone and expression. Take air direct to the opening of the bronchial tube.

A half breath is a short indrawing of breath on top of the air already in the lungs.

How long should the practice period be for beginners? — half an hour each day, — three times, not more than ten minutes at a time.

— — — —

Finish the tone but not the expiration — this continues with the same sensation that one observes when one listens intensely — that is to say, the lips remain parted and one exhales and inhales only with the diaphragm. The higher one sings, the lower one breathes. Breathing continues like a spring flows. The voice must come to the exhalation. NEVER

PUSH THE VOICE. When one sings well, one has the sensation of drinking.

— — — —

One must sing all exercises with an open throat — then the voice develops by itself. If you sing exercises with a dark (covered) tone, the voice cannot develop as it should. Later on, one can sing all tones (dark and light) with an open throat. If you begin studying the voice with dark tones only, it will be difficult to sing clear (light) tones.

— — — —

Never say to a pupil, "You sing incorrectly" or "You sing badly." You must guide the pupil's progress without his awareness of your purpose or intent. Later on it is easy to explain what you have accomplished. Never say anything too prematurely — speak only of the immediate needs, never of things to come.

— — — —

Never say anything to pupils that will confuse or discourage them (especially to women who are naturally pessimistic). Most doctors do not explain the malady to their patients.

— — — —

Sing exercises with "la" starting the tone without a "shock" or violent attack. If you throw a stone into the water, the water will splash into the air — but if you let it fall gently, it will not disturb the water — it will create only the regular undulations. When a train starts, it does not leave with a jerk — no, so gently that one does not feel the movement. When playing the violin the bow starts to descend before making the tone, and in finishing the tone the bow continues the same movement. It is similar in singing. The expiration starts before the tone (as if you have already sung) and continues after finishing the tone.

In singing a phrase or a long sustained tone one feels the force of the expiration descending little by little from the throat to the lowest extremity of the abdomen. A soprano sings the high staccato notes with the lowest muscles of the abdomen. So — if you do not have air in the bottom of the lungs, the muscles of the abdomen and of the stomach are needlessly fatigued. It is with the muscles of the abdomen and the diaphragm that one condenses the breath in the lungs. It is not necessary to have a large breath capacity (Patti and Sembrich had little) but you must know how to condense and retain the breath and not spill any of it from one tone to another — but sing the phrase like a single tone.

If you press an article in your hand forcibly, your hand will not tire very much, but if you maintain the same position without holding an object, the hand will become terribly tired and the muscles rigid.

— — — —

.It is not possible to make progress before three months have elapsed. If you progress too quickly, development is stopped (halted) for a long time. To develop, progress must be slow — step by step. If the voice progresses more quickly than the control of the breath it is necessary to stop using the voice and sing exercises silently (without tone).

— — — —

Yes, with my method the voice places itself.

— — — —

As a real gentleman never flaunts his wealth, a real voice must not display all its power. Many rich people display all their wealth, as do many singers. Keep in reserve all the extremes of your voice.

— — — —

In ascending the scales (in singing exercises) you may lift your arms — this gives strength to the muscles around the lungs.

— — — —

The throat grows stronger by itself and the tongue flattens (lowers) itself with the exercises in my method. The throat remains open throughout the whole scale. The soft palate remains high up to the head voice, when it descends to let the tone vibrate in the head. A woman must sing all exercises on "a" in the head voice.

— — — —

In order to sing, three things are essential — a voice, good health and intelligence. This method takes care of everything else. Intelligence? — that is musical intelligence, a good ear and melodic talent. If you are physically weak, it is possible to remedy the condition with exercises and time, but it is not possible to create a miracle by making a big stone out of a little stone.

— — — —

I take a voice, I make it stronger and more pleasant, etc., but if one hasn't a chest tone naturally, I cannot induce it. A dramatic soprano must have a chest tone.

— — — —

While singing, the mouth is not opened too much or too wide, but the upper lip is raised, especially at the corners.

— — — —

The breath is the ocean, — the voice is the boat which

floats on the ocean! Nature gave us the voice — we cannot change it, — but we can educate the breath and learn to control it. This — this constitutes the whole method of singing.

— — — —

The secret of the art of teaching is to wait until the pupil is ready to understand your explanation and the situation. Never burden the pupil with too much at one time. The teacher and the pupil must become so close that they think as one — like my hands (and he interlocked the fingers of both hands).

— — — —

The voice extends itself a third higher.

— — — —

From one tone to another one tightens the muscles, but not while singing a single tone!

— — — —

Those pupils who lack the patience to sing exercises exclusively for a few months, will never become singers. Those who find exercises tiresome and sing do, re, me without interest lack talent — but pupils who find beauty in all melodies have talent.

— — — —

Many people who speak with a nasal tone also sing nasally e.g. the French, because their language demands it. Many Americans and many Englishmen also speak nasally. The Italians, never! They speak with an open throat (like the Italian word "stai"). Why do the singers in Dresden sing so covered and so dark?

— — — —

The sensation while passing from one tone to another is

like listening intensely — or like having your head under water.

———

An instructor must never use the word "badly" to a pupil. He may say that the pupil sings flat. It is natural to sing flat if one does not open the mouth wide enough or if one is tired. Those who sing badly can never become singers. If one sings too sharp, it is the fault of the ear.

———

Low tones are natural, therefore do not pour (push) out too much breath while singing them. Start the tone as one starts the tone on the violin.

———

When one first learns to sing, it is necessary to sing the exercises with full voice. After the tone is firmly placed, you can sing pianissimo by economizing the breath.

———

Fast scales do much for the voice. In time you can sing slowly with the same ease. Never sing fast scales legato. In taking the breath, be careful not to lose any of the air already in the lungs.

———

The voice is like an organ. The lungs are the bellows — the throat and the mouth, the pipe. If there is too much air in the bellows the tone is bad, because the superfluous air disturbs the tone which cannot form. If the bellows have too little air, the tone is bad because the tone has not enough support.

———

As you progress, you do not listen for quantity of tone but for quality. In singing softly one finds faults more easily. At

the beginning of the study of the voice never sing pianissimo
because you squeeze (clutch) your throat.

——— ——— ——— ———

It is not possible to understand the ideas in this article*
without executing them (trying them out). If you have
always been rich you cannot really know what it means to
be poor. You must have been poor to understand poverty.

Teachers and musicians do not comprehend this — their
musical taste is sick. If I have two restaurants, one good and
one poor, I cannot realize that the good restaurant is good
unless I am a connoisseur of good food.

One hears at the opera "Oh! she has a beautiful voice!"
One never hears "How well she sings!" Many have beautiful
voices as well as beautiful figures and faces, quite naturally.
But the voice is like a flower! — presto — it's gone.

——— ——— ——— ———

Finally the voice controls the breath — not the reverse. I
have explained much in advance to you — but now let it all
come to you by itself — the legato must also come by itself.
Never drag (pull) the legato!

——— ——— ——— ———

You know what the "funicular" is, — one conveyance goes
up while the other goes down. With the first vocal sound, the
voice and the breath part at the same place — the voice going
up and the breath (energy) going down. When these forces
balance themselves, one can sing legato — one tone fuses into
the other.

——— ——— ——— ———

There are many people who can never trill. I had pupils
who sang beautifully, but could not trill. A pupil of mine

———————

*Lamperti is referring to his article "Preventing the Decadence of the Art of
Singing" (Page 1)

married a conductor who said, "No trilling! You must learn it!" She learned to trill but lost her voice.

The trill must be natural. It depends on certain nerves in the vocal cords. Without these nerves, the cords pale and lose their sonority. One can speak, but not sing.

— — — —

I have said, "Never say to a pupil, you sing badly." It is comparable to introducing someone and at the same time saying, "Take care, he is a thief." People hearing this will lock up their possessions.

— — — —

If one has a natural fault due to organic structure, for example a nasal tone, as this M——, do not try to eliminate it, for this would injure the voice. Beautify and strengthen the voice but leave the fault alone.

The celebrated baritone ——, a Frenchman, had a terrible nasality, but how he sang! Also Tamagno — all the words nasal — but what a tone!

— — — —

To sing it is necessary to have "a voice, a voice and a voice," but to sing well it is necessary to have a musical nature and to be musically intelligent.

Mr. B——, my pupil, who sang in church, was unsophisticated. He sang and played music at sight, with beautiful and fiery tone like a great singer. He was musically intelligent, and yet unworldly like a boy of fifteen.

— — — —

Start the tone at the point of the language (pronunciation). On your high notes you open your mouth too wide. Your tone is too dark. Whether you sing high or low, the resonance remains throughout in the same spot.

— — — —

In singing exercises always use "la." Then all the defects and faults will be evident. If one sings with words on dark vowels, the faults are not revealed. The syllable "la" serves like the doctor's examination of a body to find the cause of a malady.

In starting a tone, do not push. The sensation is rather that of inhaling (or drinking).

It does not matter if the high and low tones are not good at the start. In time they will become good.

— — — —

You produce too much tone. If your tone is too big, you cannot guide the voice.

Start the tone pure like a violin tone, not throatily, but on the lips. It is for this reason that the Italians said, "Tones are the flowering of the lips."

The tone is nasal because the breath is weak. You know that it is easier to speak nasally than "on the lips". Americans especially speak nasally.

— — — —

You are weak here (stomach). Your tone is too big for your breath. Your tone is like the boy in the street. With that type of tone you cannot sing with expression. It is a breathy tone (too full of air), and the tone does not vibrate like the tone of a violin. Your tone is cold. — The opera singers in Dresden sing explosively with lungs full of air and the shoulders raised.

— — — —

You are weak — the nerves of the diaphragm are weak. One can be strong, but not have the strength to sing well. One can sing well-but not have the strength for other things.

—— —— —— ——

In a portamento carry one tone to another on the sound (tone) and not on the breath (air).

—— —— —— ——

Never permit a pupil to carry the chest tones too high. There are only dark resonances in the chest.

—— —— —— ——

Why cover a tone! If it is beautiful, it is a mistake to cover it. In Italy one never permits a pupil to cover tones. They always sing like this, chiaroscuro. It is a mistake to sing too white. However, it is just as bad to sing too dark as too white.

One must sustain the tone on the lips, and let the tone vibrate in the chest (on low tones), in the mouth (for the medium tones), and the higher the tone, the higher the vibration, but the tone always remains on the lips.

—— —— —— ——

The soprano voice is like a tree. The middle voice may be pleasant and strong, but that is not essential, for it is there (on the medium) you develop the high voice. You do not water a tree at the top but at the roots, —— and the tree spreads and blooms as a natural consequence. It is the proper training of the middle voice that brings the beautiful head voice.

SELECTED ESSAYS FROM THE
WM. EARL BROWN MANUSCRIPTS

TEACHING

"I have never written a method," said my master, the younger Lamperti, "because all that a singer need know could be written on the palm of my hand. Fundamentals are three: control of powerful breath energy, trueness and ease of all tones, and distinct, correct diction, — after which a pupil unfolds according to his talent, his temperament, and his intelligence."

A teacher of singing must be master of three abilities, three modes of listening to his pupils — he should be able to hear them as they are, as they might be, and as they ought to be.

He should adjust himself and his knowledge to the talent, intelligence and temperament of each pupil.

He must beware of rules and explanations that kill spontaneity in the pupil.

He must develop the mind as well as the body.

He must help the unfolding of character.

He must arouse the desire for beauty.

"Do not let a pupil get a local habit, or a mechanical trick, but make him wait until all conditions are met and correlated. Then tone, syllable and breath become so interdependent that vibration, diction and respiration are inseparably knit together, silent or singing." (Lamperti)

A teacher should induce his pupil to be his co-worker by giving him the two tools, compressed air and focused vibration, to let him form his individual manner of singing.

Every pupil must think and reason for himself. He must daily exercise his whole body and mind. He must discover the resultant phenomena of phonation and respiration. He must feel the reciprocal relation between his body and his voice which makes possible a balance of the two factors of singing — controlled breath and pure tone.

"The singing tone evolves from the speaking voice. Do not hasten this process. Train the ear, practice vocal and physical gymnastics, and wait for the singing tone to appear spontaneously." (Lamperti)

Though relying on natural physiological facts and functions, Lamperti's teaching was remarkably free of technical detail. The following remarks were his advice to teachers:

"Teaching is like animal training! Make them jump over the stick!"

"Wait for a sign of the pupil's intelligence before giving reasons."

"Never place too much on their backs at one time!"

"Some will 'do it' yet not understand. Others will understand, yet not become great singers."

"Talent and intelligence are requisite to make the artist."

MULTICOLORED VOICE

"There are two inadequate ways of singing: too far forward in the mouth, and too far back in the pharynx — that is, too light or too dark. The normal instinctive voice is both light and dark — chiaroscuro. This multicolored voice appears when mental and physical conditions are right. It cannot be mechanically produced nor objectively controlled." (Lamperti)

Tone, though made in the throat, must reflect from the middle bones of the head toward the mouth, where it is felt as an agreeable tickling sensation on the lips. (The bones of the nose vibrate also but do not reflect the tone.)

This tone is the "chiaroscuro" (dark-light) tone of great singing. It brings to the voice the feeling of one register — a single mechanism from top to bottom. It can be opened or closed at will.

While some voices are naturally white (light) and others are congenitally somber, all singers should realize this focusing of tone in the center of the skull, from where it spreads in all directions. It will resonate automatically in head, mouth and chest, as the pitch demands.

If the point of deflection is too far back, the tone is turned toward the throat instead of toward the mouth and sounds covered. It mumbles its words. It remains dark and cannot be opened. It prevents the one register quality, and requires various unnatural mechanisms to reach high and low pitches.

Tone that reverberates directly against the teeth is too white (open). Diction may be distinct but the voice cannot be darkened (closed) at will. It also precludes the sensation of all tones starting in the same place whether high or low and also necessitates change of mechanism to obtain range or power. White tones, like covered tones, cannot be modulated without unnatural effort.

The erect poise of the head on the shoulders and the straight spine are two essentials for "chiaroscuro" singing. Tipping the head too far back while singing makes the sound too white and endangers control. Bending the head too far forward makes the tone too dark and likewise unmanageable.

"The professional singing voice must sound both dark and light and seem high in head, low in throat, and forward in mouth." (Lamperti)

SING THE SILENCES

Until silence is pregnant with tone urgent to be born, you are only making vocal noises. "Don't sing until you'd die if you didn't!" exclaimed Lamperti.

Thinking aloud musically is as subtle as thinking aloud orally. Vocal tone is delivered from silence imbued with all energies of the body, all imaginings of the mind, and all aspirations of the soul. When born, it consists of the phenomena of vibration, sounds of speech, and yearnings of the heart.

"Sing the silences! Tones sing themselves!" said Lamperti.

Thinking aloud musically on worded melodies is easier than thinking aloud orally on spoken phrases. The power of momentum and the law of continuity carry the voice from tone to tone and syllable to syllable while singing. Spoken words are spasmodic, defeating the law of continuity and the help of momentum. However, a real orator times and tempers his lines like a singer using inflections of the voice instead of melodies. He also voices the silences. "It is what we do between tones that brings real art to singing or playing," said the great master Leschetitzki to me.

"There is only one start and one stop, the beginning and the end of a song," said Lamperti.

HIGH CHEST BREATHING

There can be no "open throat" feeling unless the upper portion of the lungs is as plentifully supplied with compressed air as the lower.

A strong pressure of breath comes against shoulders and collar bone though not against the throat.

When breath is renewed at every possible opportunity, the lungs never collapse and a sensation of fixed chest results.

This is what Lamperti meant by saying, "Never use the residual air in the lungs, but only its dynamic energy. Take breath before any part of the lungs begins to collapse — even in the middle of a syllable, if in danger."

This high chest breathing must never be attained at the expense of pelvic, abdominal, diaphragmatic or intercostal participation. There is as much pressure against these confines as against the top part of the torso.

HEAD — THROAT — TORSO

Would you expect the left hand alone to produce the music of the violin?

No. It only secures the pitch of each tone in the tune.

The right hand must be trained to handle the bow until it can play on the vibrations of the string.

"You must practice with the bow until your arm drops off," exclaimed Joachim to his celebrated pupil, Maud Powell.

Well, while singing, breath is the bow. It must be completely under the control of the torso before it will "play" on the vibration in the throat.

"Breath must be a year in advance of the voice," said Lamperti.

The head and throat make nature's self-tuning, double reeded organ. It instinctively secures the pitch of each tone and the sound of each syllable of a song, if the torso competently manages respiration.

"Leave your voice alone, and train your breath," advised Lamperti.

"Great singers must be able to compress breath, hold it firmly with the abdomen, gauge its use with the diaphragm, turn it into vibration with the throat and make it bloom at the lips as tone." (Lamperti)

VOICE AND BREATH ARE AFFINITIES

Voice and breath are like two dancers who eagerly approach each other, unite, — and as one being express rhythm, melody and mood of music.

Each knows what the other is thinking, feeling and doing.

Each assists the other to cause sound to glide, to run, to leap, to pause.

Each must be expert and efficient, or one will have to carry the other as a dead-weight.

Each must act as a counterpoise to the other to keep up unbroken continuity of motion.

Each adjusts itself to the intentions and movements of the other, even when contact is momentarily broken.

Contact of voice and breath must have all the degrees of energy demanded by rhythm, melody, mood of tune and text, without violence or strain.

This association becomes so intimate and pleasurable, that all rigidity and awkwardness, all pushing and pulling cease.

The union of breath and voice "brings a sensuous delight to the whole body from head to foot, as though the body were a tongue tasting something good" (Lamperti).

Voice and breath, though individual, at last become inseparable affinities. "Tone is the upper end of breath and breath is the lower end of tone," said Lamperti.

OBJECTIVITY and SUBJECTIVITY

Tunneling from both sides, workmen finally meet in the center of a mountain.

Developing from both ends, energies finally merge in the center of the personality.

Desire for beauty of song delves on one side, technical capacity for singing labors on the other side of a talent.

Work on the mechanical side begins at the feet and extends up through pelvis, abdominal brain, diaphragm and chest to the throat.

Realizations of beauty in song begin in the skull and spread downwards through head, nostrils, mouth and pharynx to the throat.

Here desire and efficiency finally come together — talent and technique become one — the singer emerges.

When both aesthetic and practical sides of a personality touch, crass emotionalism ceases — at the same time calculated mechanism disappears.

The fact that both attributes of a talent are not equally developed accounts for the woeful lack of competent singers today. Either a talent is exploited before it matures — a facile performance being foisted on the public before it is efficient— or a gifted emotional personality crudely flaunts its feelings to the world.

Desire for beauty plus mental and physical efficiency to portray that beauty produces singing.

"Keep the heart warm and the head cool. Heart and head must go hand in hand." (Lamperti)

EDITOR'S COMMENT

I should like to add my ideas on how dynamic compressed breathing may be induced.

"Never expand the body much (in any direction) while inhaling or inherent energy of compressed breath will be weakened." (Lamperti)

Breathing in singing is like breathing in talking, but since more breath is required in singing than in speaking, it is easier to upset the balance of breath and voice while singing.

In speech, when we come to a point of depletion of the air in our lungs, we take a breath at this point of depletion. We do not pull away from this "point" and then gulp tremendous quantities of air to finish our sentence. We breathe, so to speak, through our words.

If silent breathing can be done in speech, it can also be done in singing. Sing the first phrase with the air in your mouth. Before your lungs are depleted, and *without pulling away from your waistline*, take a small, slow breath, (leaving your mouth open) breathing silently through nose and mouth. Now you have replaced the air used to sing your first phrase without having lost the residual air in your lungs. Continue doing this until the end of your song or series of exercises, breathing often to prevent any collapse of the lungs — *and always remembering not to pull away from the waistline while adding more air to the lungs.*

At first this induces a slight feeling of suffocation, so short periods of this type of breathing should be practised. As this process becomes subjective, you no longer get a suffocated sensation but a feeling that the air is renewed from within and "you breathe through your tone, getting no breath until the end of your song" (Lamperti).

At no time during the song or series of exercises must you relax while replenishing the breath, or you lose the feeling of suspension. Only when the song is over may you "let go". A comparison with tight rope walking best illustrates this. If the singer relaxes or "lets go" while replenishing the breath, it would be similar to the tight rope walker losing his balance between steps, because of too much relaxation.

This is an objective discipline and should not be practised for more than ten minutes a day. Compressed breathing cannot be coerced. Little by little, it dawns upon one how to control this quiet powerful breath energy.

"Lamperti watched the 'flowers of the lips' and literally kept his hand on the region of the solar plexus of the pupil until he felt that the diaphragm was functioning properly while both compressing breath and singing, and was assured that the reciprocal relationship between vocal utterance and breath energy brought the 'hum' into the singing-tone." (Wm. Earl Brown)

"Finally you must not think of when or how you breathe. Do you when you are speaking? Well, the same process intensified and developed a thousandfold does the singing." (Lamperti)